CHAVEZ

i

Essays from an
Asian American Perspective

Emil Guillermo

AsianWeek Books • San Francisco

Versions of the columns collected here appeared in *AsianWeek*, the national newsweekly for Asian Americans, 1995-1999.

Library of Congress Cataloging-in-Publication Data

Guillermo, Emil.
Amok!/Emil Guillermo;
Essays from an Asian American Perspective;
foreword by Ishmael Reed
p. cm.

ISBN 0-9665020-1-9

Library of Congress Catalog Card number: 99-072426

For information, contact AsianWeek Books, 809 Sacramento Street, San Francisco, CA 94108. Printed in the United States of America.

Cover and book design by John De Salvio

First AsianWeek Books Printing April 1999

For Kathy, Jilly, Dashiell, and Molly

CONTENTS

x

FOREWORD

I KNEW EMIL GUILLERMO before he went amok. Not that he was normal then, either.

I first met him at the Writers Program of Washington University at St. Louis. I was a visiting professor there. Emil was a graduate student. The year was 1979, and Emil was writing rambling works of fiction, streams of consciousness that exhibited flashes of brilliance and cutting wit. Maybe one of Emil's fictional works will be published one day.

Later, he was host of a radio show, and I remember being a guest and subjected to one of those interviews during which you don't know whether the guy is for you or against you. Just going for the truth, I suppose. I wish that other journalists would express the same kind of demeanor.

Though I believe fiction to be his gift, what has come from Emil's personal journalism is a unique and important prose voice. They show a writer at the top of his craft. A writer who refuses to be ghettoized. A writer who is capable of commenting about subjects both grand and small. Whether it be an essay about his experience as a Filipino American, affirmative action, or a wry, comic and ironic piece about Andrew Cunanan, Emil brings a perspective rarely seen in print. It's the point of view from an outspoken member of an emerging, and important group—Asian Americans. Emil's essays are part of a new chorus of concern from the fastest growing community in the country. His take on the issues, laced with his humor and attitude, makes him different from the rest.

It's that difference I find invaluable. Maybe that's because, as a Harvard-educated Filipino American, Emil has seen both the inside and outside of our society. He writes prose that turns society inside out as only one on the margins can do.

I'm happy to see this collection published. Since our first meeting, Emil has certainly paid his dues. And through it all, he's only gotten better in defining his non-fiction voice. His writing has the same conversational style that made him popular while he was the host of National Public Radio's *All Things Considered*. The fact that he's no longer there speaks more to his ouster through the machinations of an incestuous yuppie clique, rather than to any reflection of his ample talent. I remember listening to his farewell essay on NPR. It showed that he had much more class than his detractors. It was Emil at his best; eloquent, self-deprecating, humorous, and ironic.

You will not find hand-wringing in any of these essays. They are sharp, smart. Insightful and fresh. But above all, they are balanced. Even in their "amokness."

Ishmael Reed
Oakland, California

ACKNOWLEDGMENTS

I WOULD LIKE TO THANK the many people who have contributed in many different ways to the essays in this book. They deserve special mention.

My wife Kathy Guillermo, the first Guillermo to publish a book, was forever at my side, a conscientious and generous reader, editor, and friend.

My children, Jilly, Dashiell, and Molly, always kept me from going too amok. They reminded me that there's always hope for the future.

James Carroll was the ideal editor at AsianWeek. His insights and direction helped me to see as much as I could. His patience on this project allowed me to write as well as I could.

John De Salvio, book designer and friend, was a godsend. I am privileged to have him work on *Amok*.

Most of all, I'd like to thank the Fang family, the publishers of AsianWeek, who have been wonderfully supportive through the years and are most responsible for this collection. At AsianWeek, James Fang's leadership was visionary and allowed me to express my views on a variety of subjects without interference. I will always be grateful for his commitment to this project, and for his friendship.

Other people who have helped from the beginning: Florence Lewis, my English teacher at Lowell High School; Ishmael Reed, who has encouraged me from the time I met him in college to this day, to be true to my voice; Sandy Close, who consistently challenges me to see the world in new ways; Rene Cruz and Mona Lisa Yuchengko of Filipinas Magazine, and Arlyn Gajilian of the Filipino Express, for the support in the Filipino community that gave me a sense that my writing was important; and for mainstream editors like Dean Wakefield, Bob Cuddy, the late Gary McMillan, Lynn Ludlow, Tim Porter, Diane Chang, and John Flanagan, who've recognized that "Amok" had a universal message and deserved a broader audience beyond its ethnic home-base.

For all those I've inadvertently left off, due to my old age or the lapse of memory known to occur after a night of amokness, forgive me. Please know how I am indebted to your help.

One person deserves special mention at this time — my mother, Josefa, who died during the production of this book.

People who know my writing know that I derived a great deal from my mom. With my father Emiliano's passing in 1978, my mother remained my connection to history and culture and all things Filipino to the day she died. While her loss momentarily delayed the finish of this book, it is with the strength of her spirit that it is completed.

Ultimately, it is to the memory of both my mother and father, Josefa and Emiliano, and the richness of their lives as first generation Asian American immigrants of Filipino descent that this book is dedicated.

Emil Guillermo

INTRODUCTION

Why *Amok*?

Amok with a "k" is a phonetic bastardization of the root word, *amoq*, a Malay term that has terrified many. As an Asian American of Filipino descent, I heard my relatives refer to it under a different name: *juramentado*. But I knew what they meant. It was a kind of "craziness," but with purpose. It involved knives and bleeding, generally. But *juramentado* takes up too much space on a smallish book cover, forcing an unnatural cropping of my picture. Therefore, we go straight to the authentic root word—*amoq*.

Amoq can be noun or verb. It can describe an individual or his state of mind. It is a far-out state, farther than the Philippines, which was never even a state, just a colony. One can be *amoq*. Or one can be in the process of becoming *amoq*. Or one is transported, i.e., one can "go *amoq*." Or as is often the case, one can "run *amoq*." Note: A "walking *amoq*" is an aberration and should be reported to the police immediately.

Amoq can also simply describe a person's behavior, the true defining moment, an act specific and undeniable. As described in William Marsden's 18th-century Malay dictionary, an *amoq* is one who engages "furiously in battle, attacking with desperate resolution, rushing in a state of frenzy to the commission of indiscriminate murder."

That's my kind of word.

But relax. There's nothing to fear here except the death of a few old notions and stereotypes about Asian Americans.

Docile? Demure? No more. And what about their driving? Well, "Amok" is the middle name on my driver's license.

Recently, the media have developed a fondness for the concept, as in "political correctness run amok," a handy phrase to describe anything the white media doesn't agree with. Compassion? Well that's "political correctness run amok." So is the move for diversity in schools, or demands for affirmative action in the corporate world, or any call for fairness, justice, etc. But this use of amok as metaphor shows a basic misunderstanding of the word. "Political correctness run amok" sounds more like a virus. Amokness always begins with the individual, is self-induced, and always involves a frenetic act of violence. It's loud, somewhat suicidal, and yet unusually self-affirming. It's a cultural trance that puts one in a state to do the impossible, like fight an armed colonizer with only a stick. Amokness gives one the courage and the power to strike the transgressor. It is a unique method of Asian assertion.

In 1991, when I began writing essays and columns in the ethnic media, I decided to take back the word from the anti-PC types and make it my metaphor. My real inspiration was *Aieeee!*, the historical collection by Asian American fiction writers in the '70s led by Frank Chin and Sean Wong. *Aieeee!* is the universal sound of Asian American anguish that ran throughout the anthology. It broke the silence of a curious but cautious community and revealed stories of the culture that existed right under all our noses.

Aieeee! filled the void in fiction. *Amok* intends to fill the void in general. When President Clinton began the exercises known as Town Halls on Race, he practically had to beg an Asian American to come forward to say anything. The community's reticence has been legendary. *Amok* ends the silence and presents an Asian American perspective in the public arena of ideas and commentary, a literary realm where Asian Americans have been either marginalized or ignored.

Certainly, Asian Americans have had a hand in their own silence. To speak out, to be a "public Asian" is almost considered anti-Asian in some community circles. To these folks, silence is becoming. One learns to live flying under the radar. One begins to accept that as a person of color, one is essentially a member of an "underground society" in American democracy. Invisible. Non-participants. It's good enough for most.

Yet it's clear that as American society grows more diverse, with Asian Americans as the fastest growing ethnic group, silence is no longer an option. There comes a time when silence is no longer prudent, and one must in some way, "go amok." There's a different threshold for everyone. For some, it will be the urge to rebut a few misguided politicians and media folk. For others, it will be the moment of another injustice, no matter how slight, of an Asian American.

For those of an older generation, silence will still be golden. But for younger Asian Americans, the flash point is lower. They've seen the history and don't want to re-live it. They've come to a point where things cannot be left as they are, issues not addressed, feelings left unsaid. Limits are about to be reached. There's been too much pent-up inside. Like a bamboo steamer whose lid must come off, one is transported into a state of amokness.

It's about to happen on a grand scale. As Asian Americans grow to 10 million in this country, amokness is an outcome of the community's coming of age. In the years ahead, you will see more Asian Americans making a difference, coming out of the shadows, into prominence, going amok. And it's about time.

So the question comes up? *Why "Amok?"* As we go into the next century, demographers point to the future when "so-called minorities" become the "majority." It's already happened in California. Whites dipped to 49.7% in the state in 1998. The Asian population in the state is at 4 million, 12% of the state's 32 million people. To those still locked into a black/white paradigm, Asians outnumber blacks by 2-1. When you add the Latino population — 31.3% of the state's population — it's clear. America's future is now in the New California.

If anyone is concerned about the issue of race in the new millennium, it's time they understood the Asian American part of the equation. The ethnic press has been and continues to be the historical record of the community's public discourse. The writing in "Amok" reflects where many Asian Americans stood when we were considered too small, too quiet, too docile. We weren't silent. Just ignored. There was an amok voice that challenged the notion of our invisibility. This volume gives readers a sense of where we were and where we must go if we are to solve the race dilemmas of a new era together.

1

All About Me

I WAS TOO YOUNG FOR VIETNAM. My 'Nam was Harvard. While there, I suffered the Harvard version of post-traumatic stress, which is far superior to what you'd find at even the best public university.

One way to relieve the stress was to bring my family from San Francisco to Cambridge for my graduation. In their own way, they needed to graduate too. As Americans. But for them, the memorable moment came on a side trip to New York. For my Filipino immigrant parents, who had never been east of Reno, this was a big deal. And aside from the pomp and circumstance, there was really just one thing they wanted to do on the "Right Coast": take a boat ride to the Statue of Liberty.

On a gray, hazy summer day we took an immigrant's journey, a drive down from Boston and then a boat ride on ferry that circles Manhattan. There we were, as if on a victory lap, the "American Family" triumphant. West Coast immigrants come east, son graduating from an elite bastion, riding a boat around the capital of the world. My mom, my sister, me, and my Dad, all beaming. We asked a stranger to capture the moment with my sister's Instamatic. Our Edward Weston framed Lady Liberty perfectly, but we were in motion and the final image is of the torch coming out of my father's head. It's my favorite photograph—a snapshot of the American Dream.

Harbard Man, Class of '77
Finding one's own way in spite of the credentials

B ill Gates was in the Harvard Class of '77. So was I. I graduated. He didn't. I guess I showed him.

Yes, this is the week that the 1,600 members of the Class of 1977 hold their 20-year reunion. The 20th is the gut check. It's not like the 25th, the big money year, when the college has you back so that it can ask you to make your big donation; and oh, by the way, does little Johnny want to live in Harvard Yard someday?

No, the 20th isn't the shakedown. It's more like a wake-up call, to see what happened to the class. And to get you ready for the 25th, Harvard reminds you it's time to get to work. There are just five more years before you bring your checkbook.

But the Class of '77 turned out to be special. It wasn't clear at first. We were the tail-end of the boomer generation, the part of the generation that missed the war and had practically nothing exciting to protest at graduation.

As it turned out, that set us up perfectly for the go-go '80s. Most of us went in without protest. We were on the cusp of the Reagan years, on the verge of the time when greed and avarice were openly embraced. We were free of the moral dilemma of Vietnam. We could do and get for ourselves. So what's the big surprise that Gates—the richest man in America—was in Harvard's Freshman Register? (And to think, we were both in the G's.)

Others in the class certainly tried to be the richest men and women in the country. The current "class book," a simple-looking red-covered measuring stick for alums, reads like a "Who's Who," or at least, a "Who's Conventional" of CEOs and COOs, presidents, and executive vice presidents. Investment bankers. Lots of them.

2

People who never met a merger and acquisition they didn't like. A pretty fair harvest of elites.

There are also doctors. Psychiatrists. Surgeons. And lawyers. Tons of lawyers. The best of them are like my former college roommate Nick Carlin from Berkeley. He's smart enough to play bass in a reggae band. He's one of the cool people in the class. Like Stephen Chao, the Asian American Fox network executive who got fired by Rupert Murdoch for sending in a male stripper to perform at a meeting of television executives. Cool is relative.

Oh, the class isn't just one success story after another. There's a guy who lists his last known address as a state prison. Then there are the classmates who are dead.

And then there's me.

I must admit, I admire the hell out of Bill Gates. Not only do I have a pretty decent computer operating system that just corrected a major disk failure, but Gates has also lifted a burden off every person in my class. Now I don't have to make all the money in the world. Bill has it. I can just call Bill every now and then to make sure it's all safe. And then I can spend the rest of my time pursuing the things money can't buy.

But I admire him for another reason. He's made everyone in the class think of where they are and what they're doing. Judging from the comments in the class book, the specter of Gates has made people examine the greed in their lives. They've discovered values. They're spending time with their kids, their families. Spending less time at work. Bill Gates has been good for the family values of the Class of '77.

And he's done it by going his own way. He didn't graduate, remember? Though it may not show, I did. Even back then, when he dropped out and followed his vision, he knew the secret. In some ways, I'm just trying to be like Bill. I've spent the last 20 years trying to forget I went to Harvard. And trying to stay on the path of my own making.

The fact is, if you go to Harvard, you're supposed to become one of the aforementioned archetypes of success, whether or not that's who you really are. And if you were on a scholarship, then there's some pressure to reward the benefactor by following the standard path.

Admittedly, for a Filipino kid from San Francisco's Mission District, Harvard can be useful. It's an equalizer of sorts. Like carrying a small atom bomb. When people look at me and make an assumption based on race—when discrimination takes place—Harvard is always a handy thing to detonate.

But the fact is, for me, "Harvard as weapon" has been more gratifying than my memory of "Harvard as a total experience." For a person of color, Harvard was not the best place to be in the '70s. It's become better. In my day, Harvard was an isolating place that provided me with a mixed experience both academically and socially.

Harvard did not fail me totally. I went there and learned a little Asian American history, specifically Filipino immigration to America. Oddly, I had to go 3,000 miles from the largest enclave of Asian Americans to learn how to become more Filipino.

And that provided me with the foundation for my own affirmative action. It came as I delivered the Ivy Oration during graduation week. Traditionally, the Ivy is the speech that pokes fun at Harvard. I was the first Filipino to have the honor. So I declared to the 5,000 or so assembled in Harvard Yard in my best Fliponics (my Filipino version of Ebonics): "I am a Har-BARD man!"

This made the people very uncomfortable. What was this brown guy speaking in a pidgin tongue doing at our celebration? Since when does the valet get to give a speech?

4

But then I told them that the four years had done the trick. And though I may still look and act Filipino, at long last, with every ounce of ethnic pride in my body, I could finally proclaim in my whitest sounding broadcast voice that I was a "Har-Vard man!"

The tension broke and a cloudburst of laughter exploded. The predominantly white crowd was relieved. They saw me as one of them.

But I knew better. I wasn't.

While I've enjoyed the fruits of affirmative action and appreciate the opportunities, I know there is a bitter flip side that people of color often fail to recognize: that affirmative action can work as a form of cultural imperialism.

Ultimately, I realized I couldn't begin my life until I was strong enough to reject Harvard's well-defined patterns for success. Twenty years later, I have no regrets. Thanks, but no thanks. I'm just happy being my own man.

Just like Bill.

June 6, 1997

Mom's Sundae

When my favorite 'resident alien' turned citizen

We were eating ice cream at Blum's, the now defunct San Francisco shrine to the sweet tooth. Just me and my Mom, or—in homeboy-speak, using the pop grammar of endearment—me and my Moms.

There was only one of her. But she was definitely in possession of something: citizenship.

That's why we were celebrating, with traditional American food of the high-cal, high-fat nature. Forget apple pie. This was an ice cream sundae to end all ice cream sundaes, double-scooped, a massive squiggle of

5

whipped cream, chocolate syrup, with a cherry on top. Mom was an American. At last.

I'll never forget that scene. It's my Norman Rockwell moment.

That was more than 10 years ago, significant because Mom was in her 70s, a widow and a resident alien. As a kid I always thought that was funny because it reminded me of my then-favorite TV show, My Favorite Martian. Whenever I saw that, I thought of Mom, my favorite "resident alien." She wasn't Donna Reed. Or Lucy. She was Ray Walston.

Aliens had special status back then when green cards were really green. They could do just about anything citizens could do. Anything we needed to do. Shop. Take the bus. "And they won't arrest me," she'd say. And we'd laugh, except during those times when she didn't let me have my way, and I wished they'd knock on our door and send her back. Why shouldn't I stay up late? I may have been seven at the time, but at least I was a citizen.

I always lost those power plays. Mom's domain was the home. And it trumped democracy.

I always thought she was just fine as your common, everyday, garden-variety green card holder. Everyone was nice to her. No one looked down on her. No one made fun of her. Except for my Dad.

My Dad would joke using his best Filipino accent that Mom wasn't a "ceeteezin." He was a citizen. He came from the Philippines in the 1920s. And he wore his citizenship like a set of suspenders. Especially on election day.

He'd go out and vote the way the cook's union told him. And Mom just figured it was the family vote. She stayed at home and took care of me and my sister. That's what she was used to. Being an alien was all right by her.

So you can imagine my surprise when she declared to

my sister and me that she was "taking her oath." She would renounce her place of birth, the Philippines, and finally accept America as her home.

"Mom, you've been an alien almost 40 years," I said.

"Yeah," she said. "And Reagan's been president for three."

My father had died just as Reagan took office. It left my Mom on a widow's pension. Social Security. My mom was hardly one of Reagan's welfare queens. She lived frugally, and qualified for the free food programs that provided chunks of cheese the size of ottomans. No one could eat cheese fast enough.

Clearly, the good times were over. Reagan cut taxes, stripped spending, and installed his "trickle down" theories. But Mom knew nothing would trickle down to her. Citizenship was the only way to fight against any further erosion.

"I have to vote now," she told me.

It turned out, after all these years, my Mom had Susan B. Anthony's spirit after all.

The only thing to trickle down to Mom was a politicized anger. And a wicked sense for "John Hinckley as Hero" jokes. Nothing like a John Hinckley joke to make you appreciate the First Amendment.

As we approach Mother's Day, I've got to hand it to my Mom. She had the vision. She knew something was happening back then. She knew better than the McLaughlin Group. There was trouble ahead. She took action. She now collects her Social Security with pride, in the name of FDR, my father, and all that's good about America. It's barely enough to get by.

Today, I'm seeing my Mom's motivation replicated en masse by the hundreds who are rushing to become citizens. I walked down to the INS offices in San Francisco and couldn't believe the busloads of people lined up just to get through the revolving glass door. Before it shuts. Since my Mom became an American, she's slowed down considerably. So has Reagan. But Congress hasn't. Last week's Senate vote on welfare cuts for non-citizens was a milestone in immigrant history. It marked the formalization of this new era of scapegoating, one that we've come to expect over the last few years. The bill not only targets illegal immigrants, but also targets legal immigrants—green card holders, resident aliens, people who receive public assistance.

Few will speak out for illegal immigrants these days. Illegal is illegal, right? But how moral is taking away benefits from legal residents of this country who are needy for reasons of age or disability.

I'd hate to think about my mother's medical bills these last few years if she were not eligible for all the state and federal aid. Thank God my Mom's a citizen. She can get sick all she wants. She might even get sick from this legislation.

These mean-spirited cutbacks are driven by the idea that legal immigrants cost more in government benefits than they pay in taxes. But keep in mind only about five percent of working-age legal immigrants receive public assistance.

Immigrants aren't bankrupting our country. Legislators are bankrupt ethically to deny aid to legal residents, specifically resident aliens. America has always been about we, the people. Not we, the citizens.

My mom knows that. She read it in the Constitution.

May 10, 1996

Father's Game
Learning the score with Dad

I am coming up to my seventh Father's Day. I can tell by the number of coffee mugs I own that say "World's Greatest Dad." These are not Pulitzer Prizes. They aren't even World Cups. But considering the awards committee (my three kids), the mugs are more satisfying.

My daughter chooses mugs. But perhaps yours is into ties or socks, putters or chain saws. Whatever the award medium, we dads must accept all items graciously.

I, however, know just how unworthy I am. I still feel like a stand-in on Father's Day. For the seventh straight year, the mug might say "World's Greatest Dad," but deep down I know I'm still just "Rookie of the Year."

For me, Father's Day will never be absolutely mine. It will still belong to my Dad. If you are the Americanized son of an Asian immigrant, you know what that means. We still owe them. For all the lost Father's Days.

My Dad spoke Ilocano. This is what Marcos spoke, but without the power. He spoke English too. But I spoke it better. It made our "relationship" a quiet one. The only time we really connected was when watching baseball. He had an immigrant's passion for the game. It symbolized America with its anthem and heroism. And it was a patient game. The language of balls and strikes was easy, the math even simpler: three strikes, four balls, three outs, nine innings.

My Dad was many innings older than me—50 years worth. I remember when he taught me how to play. He brought me out to San Francisco's Golden Gate Park— the Panhandle—an appropriate name, I thought, for a fry cook and his son to learn to play ball.

It was a simple lesson. He handed me that bat, and

threw the ball at me. He wasn't a great teacher. But that's when he knew to call in tutors. We'd go to Candlestick and sit in the grandstands to see Willie Mays, with whom my father shared a first name, if not his statistics.

Baseball gave us a context. "What's the score?" one of us would always ask. One of us would always know. We followed the score. We had a stake in the team, and in each other. But of course, there were seasons when not even baseball would save us. Before I was out of junior high school, my father had retired, and I was going to father-son events alone. He was old. By age 12, I was an ageist.

We kept drifting apart, our lives as patterned as a baseball diamond. He was the first-base line, I was the third-base line—a field apart, connected only at home.

But then I went to college on the East Coast. Though I majored in alienation, I took a few courses where I learned a little about the hardship and racism endured by Filipino immigrants in the '20s. I learned about the links between the exclusion laws and the general anti-Asian sentiment at the time, that were codified by such things as the anti-miscegenation laws.

I never understood why my father, after coming to America in 1927, lived a bachelor's life until the '50s. I had thought it was by choice, preference, inability, or for lack of social skills. I thought it might have something to do with his penchant for loud ties. It never dawned on me that he stood out like a loud tie. It was more than just fate. It was society. History taught me that, and through it, I found a clear path to my father. It was a little late, but it set up our ninth inning perfectly.

On the Wednesday before Father's Day 1978, we did a day game. My treat. We were a striking pair. I was wearing a jacket and tie, so we got a discount saying I was a businessman. He was in a Giants cap and running shoes, and acting like a rascal—cutting in line, running about, me in tow. I had to apologize to the ticket person as I paid for our seats. They cost a buck-fifty to sit in left field. But the little guy wanted to sit closer. So we snuck down past the guard and wound up in prime third-base territory.

During the game, we enjoyed our passion quietly. Fancying myself a broadcaster, I was doing play-by-play in my head. Every now and then, I would turn to Dad for a little color. He was involved with the drama himself, in between bites of his homemade adobo sandwich—vinegary pork bits on white bread, tastier than a ballpark frank.

The Giants celebrated our outing with a fine performance. They fought back to take the lead from the Phillies. And then it was up to Vida Blue to mow them down in the bottom of the ninth. Blue, no longer in his prime and written off by many as an old man in his 30s, struck out both Greg Luzinski and Mike Schmidt, the heart of the order, to end the game.

We stood and yelled together in wild appreciation, which led to our only real conversation of the day. Would the Giants get through June and go all the way? My Dad was willing to take a psychic flyer on that one. "They'll go all the way now," he said.

As it was, the Giants didn't. And two hours later, back home, after he saw the future and the highlights on the local news, my father died on that Wednesday before Father's Day. Hardening of the arteries, the doctor said. But deep in my heart, I knew it was Pennant Fever.

June 16, 1995

2

Your Papers, Please

I **WAS BORN HERE,** but I look like I could be one of them. I've even been asked for my papers.

I was on a bus getting into Philadelphia. A man came up and looked me in the eye. He actually uttered the phrase. My papers? Which one did he want, the Boston Globe or the New York Times? All I knew is that he wasn't taking the "Sports" until I was done.

Fear of immigrants has been up and down, like the stock market. In fact, when Americans are doing well, society tends to be more benevolent. But when Americans are fearful of losing their jobs, it's the fault of those damn immigrants. We'll blame everything on them.

The fact is, it's all linked to our fear and lack of self-esteem as Americans. We're not very big-hearted when we feel small.

How do we feel now? If the anti-immigrant sentiment happens to be down now, it may be because people finally realize that the New Americans are a large and vital part of society that can't be scapegoated. But just wait. The national mood will change, and the issue will back. It always is when we feel less assured, less secure, and less confident about what being an American means.

Open Borders

Legal, and flipping burgers

Have you ever noticed how hard it is for people to come to this country legally?

I have a cousin who came here in the '60s. Once he was established, he petitioned for his sister and three brothers in the late '70s. It seemed like a good deal. They were hard working, industrious adults from the Philippines in their late 40s and 50s. They were in their prime.

But then they got their papers and were told to wait their turn—essentially, they had to put their American Dream on hold. The dream got them through martial law.

Sixteen years later, my cousins are finally here. They're older now. One is almost ready to retire. But the others are offtrack, lost in America, and doing jobs that are clearly beneath them. Three of them flip burgers in the fast-food industry. Their dream is to be captains of french fries one day. Maybe they should have gone illegal. Can't be any worse of a crime than what's happening to them now.

Break the law? Well, tell me who's the victim? People come here for economic opportunity. They don't come here to be on the dole. If anything, they get jobs, pay taxes, and lead productive lives. Yes, there are tons of undocumenteds sitting in state pens around the country. They've all committed crimes. And we're not talking illegal entry. We're talking murder and robbery. Before you say, "Look at all those illegal alien criminals!" as if there were a real correlation between criminality and illegal immigration, consider how many more people sit in jail who are bona-fide citizens. You can send back the real undocumented criminals. The rest we should keep. They're human resources.

14

That's why overstaying a visa sounds like a decent thing. It's more efficient that way, and probably better overall for everyone. In fact, you could get right into the economy as a taxpaying member of society, and you'd be thriving—unlike my legal cousins, who are trying to figure out if there's any real difference between a Big Mac and a Whopper.

Compare overstaying with some current proposals. Congress, for example, is talking about a bill that would make it harder for families to be united. So much for family values. Clearly, penalizing families is not the way to go. But in the event that you still feel uncomfortable about overstaying visas, here's an even better idea:

Why don't we just let them all in? I'm not talking about amnesty or legalization. I'm talking about open borders. Come on down!

That's what President Clinton should have said in his State of the Union address. That would have been gutsy.

Instead, the president went into "get tough" mode. "We are increasing border controls by 50 percent," he said. Then he delivered his supposed bombshell: "We're increasing inspections to prevent the hiring of illegal immigrants. And tonight, I announce I will sign an executive order to deny federal contracts to businesses that hire illegal immigrants."

It was greeted by 17 seconds of applause from politicians who know that the general public hates those dastardly illegal immigrants, everyone's favorite scapegoats.

But let's give Clinton at least 17 seconds of credit. Any law that cracks down on employers who hire illegals and says, "The boss is toast," is at least on the right track. Since 1986, Congress has made it illegal to hire undocumenteds, but as we all know, enforcement has been lax. So much for our nation of laws.

Laws? No one cared. Said Alan Nelson, onetime commissioner of the Immigration and Naturalization Service, of the 1980s, "The attitude of the time was that illegal immigration was OK."

So now the president wants to enforce these laws. But how effective will this be? The penalty is the denial of federal contracts, but unless some garment shop gets a big order to whip up some school uniforms to be distributed by the president to public schools, who cares about federal contracts? I wonder how many among the traditional industries that employ illegal workers (construction, food processing, hotels, etc.) rely on federal contracts as their bread and butter.

Frankly, I'd say a lot of the illegals are coming in through people who don't care about federal contracts. I really doubt that the first mate of the Golden Venture was on a government contract.

Still, the president isn't as bad as California governor Pete Wilson. Wilson goes so far as to bash illegal immigration on the one hand, and then turn around and veto bills that go after the employers that exploit the undocumented on the other.

If our top lawmakers have such a hard time figuring out which side of the immigration laws suit them, is it any wonder that someone could get the idea that overstaying a visa would be just fine?

Which brings me back to my better idea: open the borders and let people in. Crazy? Conservative/libertarian groups like the Cato Institute think it's a grand idea. They're sensitive to the issue of privacy rights and national ID cards for everybody. They're worried about big brother.

The Libertarians tend to take the lead on issues like this but rank-and-file conservatives tend to follow suit. For example, Libertarians have long been for legalizing drugs. Just this week William F. Buckley's National

Review argued that the war on drugs is a waste of resources and that drugs should be made legal.

How long do you think it'll be before the other conservatives follow suit on immigration? The INS is one of the few areas in the budget that's getting an increase—of $130 million. And you know how everyone bad mouths Big Government these days. Cracking down on illegals is an absolute waste. But certainly not as great a waste as seeing my cousins wait 16 years to get burger jobs.

January 26, 1996

The New Eco Villains

A shift in the environmental debate

There was so much hot air at the Greenhouse Gas meetings in Japan this week, one wonders if the talks themselves had an adverse impact on the ozone layer.

The problem is that any binding treaty to reduce greenhouse gas emissions will come at a price. And who wants to pay for mending that big hole in the ozone?

Will it be the developing countries in Asia, Africa, and Latin America? Countries on those continents emit just 27 percent of the world's carbon dioxide. Or will the richer industrialized countries pay? The United States, Europe, Russia, and Japan emit 73 percent of the gases.

It is already becoming a rich vs. poor class battle between nations. Of course, anything the good green politicians agree to will be passed on to businesses and individuals.

As we all know, everyone wants a pollution-free environment, but nobody wants to pay for it. It is the basic dynamic of the environmental debate. Who's to blame? Who's to pay? But no matter how hot it gets during the

Japan talks, it's going to get even hotter in the United States.

That's because the environmental debate in this country is shifting from class to race. We're about to find out how green our racism is.

This month, ballots are being prepared for mailing to more than 500,000 members of the Sierra Club, the nation's oldest and largest environmental organization. The members will vote on a proposal to endorse a policy to reduce annual immigration to the United States from the current ceiling of 900,000 to a much reduced 200,000.

The drive is spearheaded by Alan Kuper, a retired engineering professor from Cleveland and a Sierra Club member for 24 years. "How can we protect America's anything ... if we don't deal with the rapidly growing U.S. population?" he said to the Los Angeles Times. "The underlying cause of our environmental problems is too many people, and everybody knows that. But it is so difficult to talk about."

Indeed it is. Such a noble sounding cause. I can see Mr. Kuper now standing as proud and as tall as the Statue of Liberty next to that great environmental disaster known as Lake Erie. He's like a man who doesn't know what he has done. He just used immigrants as a scapegoat for all of our environmental sins.

And what a great solution. The United States alone emits 25 percent of all greenhouse gases but makes up just four percent of the world population.

We could be asking our corporations to help out. We could also be looking at our own habits. According to Californians for Clean Air Progress, the average car emits 441 pounds of pollutants each year. Carpooling just once a week is said to reduce smog by eight tons a day in the San Francisco Bay Area alone.

But why cramp our lifestyle? Why should we blame

ourselves for pollution when we can blame people who aren't even in this country! American Corporations? They must be saints. Individuals who don't carpool or recycle? Exemplary. But Immigrants? The New Environmental Villains!

Who's kidding whom? Kuper and his Sierra Club cohorts are engaging in no less than environmental demonizing.

Why cut back living the American way? Just blame the immigrants. As certain Sierra Club-types like Kuper see it, immigrants are some kind of toxic citizen contaminating the environment. Reducing their entry means more for us Americans, and a guilt-free, pain-free way to go green. The more racist you are, the greener you get. But is the movement really racist?

Certainly, the Sierra Club proposal is a form of de facto racism. The Sierra Club will go after legal immigrants. Not illegal ones. Not the paper-fearing, bureaucracy-beguiling, undocumented ones. The reduction will come from those who actually had faith in the system and have endured the arduous INS process in order to be reunited with family in the U.S.

These are people who played by the rules and still face a wait of up to 20 years to enter the United States legally. All immigrants are lumped together. The Sierra Club wants to shut the borders, keep the clean air in, and keep the immigrants out.

Who are these immigrants? According to the most recent figures from the INS, the top five countries of origin are Mexico, the Philippines, Vietnam, the Dominican Republic, and China.

This ballot measure allows many to see the dark side of the environmental movement for the first time. Actually, the Sierra Club considered the same question two years ago, but a national vote was derailed. This time, Kuper collected more than 2,200 signatures to get a vote. The success of the petition was not surprising considering the strong link between some environmentalists and anti-immigration groups.

The Federation of American Immigration Reform was started in 1978 by John Tanton, a former Sierra Club executive director. This new ballot measure brings together Sierra Club forces with the California Coalition for Immigration Reform, a co-sponsor of the infamous Proposition 187—the proposal to deny benefits to illegal immigrants.

Is green so good?

One thing is for sure, green is white. Lily white. Snow white. Cirrus cloud white. The Sierra Club says that seven percent of its membership considers itself a member of an ethnic group. This new push to restrict immigration won't be good for community public relations.

You want to get a Gomez or a Liu to carpool? Better not let them know you're for blocking their uncle or aunt or cousin from joining the family. Coming from countries where being green takes a back seat to basic survival, the Sierra Club is not bound to help in minority outreach.

In fact, this Sierra Club ballot will only serve to exacerbate environmentalists' overall lack of concern for minority communities. Let's face it, most low-income ethnic communities have been accepted dumping grounds for industrial pollution.

In California, change seemed forthcoming with the passage of the Environmental Quality Act, a bill that would have identified and mitigated high pollution levels in minority and low-income areas. The Natural Resources Defense Council called it a long overdue effort to incorporate considerations of equity and fairness in the administration of our environmental laws.

What happened? Gov. Pete Wilson vetoed the bill in October. Where was the Sierra Club's high-powered lobby? Speaking on behalf of people of color? Not likely.

It doesn't help the overall legislative process for people of color when an influential, progressive organization like the Sierra Club starts spouting off anti-immigrant rhetoric. This is the Sierra Club, for chrissakes, not the National Rifle Association. Is hating immigrants now politically correct?

The group could go a lot further by pursuing the real resource robbers. Step up the crackdown on corporate sinners and modern lifestyles. Need more controversy? Take on birth control. Speak out against multiple births. Pass out condoms and diaphragms. Demonize Iowa's McCaugheys! Seven kids and not a cloth diaper on any of them.

But scapegoating immigrants in the name of the environment? That's racism. Come January, Sierra Club members should vote their conscience. Being a tree hugger shouldn't give rise to nativism.

December 4, 1997

Two Strikes, You're Out
An immigrant's tale

There's nothing worse than being a murderer. Except for maybe being an immigrant. Or possibly both.

My friend Fred knows all too well. So does his wife, Remy, and their two kids. Recently, we sat down to a family dinner, a veritable Sunday night Filipino feast. Everything was in place. The sinigang (soup), the adobo (stew), the pansit (noodles). But a somber atmosphere prevailed. A person was missing. Remy's father, Pedro.

21

"He's back in the Philippines," Remy told me. "The INS already deported him."

She looked down at her plate and held back tears. "We were going to go get him at the INS holding center this weekend. But they just put him on a plane and sent him back. They didn't even call us or anything."

Pedro Ablao's problem? He was an immigrant convicted of murder. Involuntary manslaughter.

"That means it wasn't pre-meditated," said my friend Fred. "He just went amok, I guess."

It was back in September 1992. Pedro was a 58-year-old, law-abiding green-card holder, an immigrant of good standing for more than 14 years. From day one he was never a burden to American society. Typically Filipino, he was a hard-working man gainfully employed in the restaurant service industry. He lived a modest life within a narrow world of family and relatives. But it was still superior to life in the Philippines. It was his American Dream.

Then it all came crashing down. A domestic dispute erupted with his wife, Salvacion. Why were they fighting? No one knows. Too much bliss? Or not enough? In the end, she was dead, and the bloody knife was Pedro's.

His lawyers claimed self-defense. There were cuts on his hand, suggesting a vigorous battle with wife and knife. It convinced a jury that Pedro Ablao was not Jack the Ripper. Not Charlie Manson. Not even Squeaky Fromme. They found him guilty of the lesser charge, involuntary manslaughter, and sent Pedro to state prison.

Pedro served less than four years, and was set for release. But a funny thing happened while he sat quietly in the Big House. The outside world was undergoing a change. Pedro Ablao was falling victim to politics. Prop. 187 emerged like bad mold. It spoiled the dream and turned immigrants into scapegoats. Though 187 is still being held up in the courts, one piece of legislation got through. And it's enough to wreck a person's life: The Anti-Terrorism and Effective Death Penalty Act of 1996. President Clinton signed it into law on the first anniversary of the Oklahoma City bombing. It was intended to make it easy to deport immigrants suspected of terrorism. Too bad the perpetrators of the Oklahoma bombing now appear to be home-grown terrorists Timothy McVeigh and Terry Nichols. Real Americans. And to think, most everyone thought it was the work of foreigners.

But that fact didn't force a change in the law. If anything the INS has used the law to go after immigrants with a vengeance. The law does, after all, allow for wholesale deportations. And in an anti-immigrant era, that's what you call "pleasing the public." In just one year, the increase in criminal and noncriminal deportations has gone up nearly 30 percent to an estimated 93,000 nationwide.

In the meantime, the knee-jerk law is causing real terror in immigrant households in America. The victims of the new law are legal immigrants, permanent residents with green-card status who have been convicted of an "aggravated felony." These are crimes like theft, fraud, drug offenses, and, in Pedro Ablao's case, involuntary manslaughter.

The new law is harsher than harsh. Some lawyers complain it doesn't even matter when the crime was committed. The INS is enforcing the law retroactively. Commit a crime? So what if you do the time? If you're an immigrant, the clock's still ticking. If you're an aggravated felon and an immigrant, that's two strikes, buddy. And under the new rules, it's "Two strikes, you're out." Literally. Deported. No appeal, no hearing. It's not just un-American, it's practically sub-American, unfairly being applied only to legal immigrants. Rights? Constitution? What constitution?

Pedro Ablao found out that the new law means business. Last September, at age 62, Pedro was set for release from prison. He served his time, paid the price for his crime, and looked forward to seeing Fred, Remy, and his grandchildren. Instead, with the new law in effect, Pedro was immediately placed in the custody of the INS. It shuttled him back and forth between holding facilities in Los Angeles and Arizona for nearly a year.

"They treated him better in prison," Fred told me. "He had lost weight. His health was bad. His eyes had cataracts. They didn't give him the treatment he needed."

Desperately trying to help his father-in-law, Fred consulted an attorney. But the attorney, Danny Flynn, let him know there was nothing that could be done. The INS was detaining him legally. The new law not only prohibited release on bond pending hearings, it eliminated any hearings in federal court.

It was absolute. It was Kafkaesque. If Pedro fights the deportation, the new law trumps. If he returns to the Philippines, he faces members of his wife's side of the family known to seek retribution. Already, he's received death threats. If he goes back, and returns to the U.S., despite his green card, his entry would be illegal, subjecting him to a mandatory 15 years in prison. Wrote the lawyer to my friend: "Seems like [Pedro's] only hope is to win on appeal [in immigration court] or wait out favorable changes in the law."

Neither is likely. So much for justice.

At this point, a case pending in the 9th Circuit Court of Appeals is testing whether Congress can strip the courts of the power to hear deportation cases. But a decision isn't expected for weeks, if not months. And then similar cases are expected to be filed throughout the different circuit courts in the country. Ultimately, the Supreme Court will rule on the law. But by then, considering his health, Pedro Ablao could be dead.

For now, he's back in the Philippines for the first time in 20 years, living in fear. He's separated from the support of his immediate family in the U.S.: Fred, Remy, and his grandchildren—all part of an old dream he can now barely remember.

"It's so unfair," Fred told me at the dinner table. "He's not a threat to anyone. He's a soft-spoken guy. We have vicious murderers set free every day who are walking the streets. But Pedro, being an immigrant, gets deported. It's just not fair."

After four years in prison, Pedro Ablao got a face full of the political wind. He's an immigrant who had one bad day on which he did one terrible thing. An immigrant who committed a crime, "an aggravated felony." Two strikes. In today's America, that's all you get.

October 3, 1997

The Racism Within Us

Anti-Asian bigotry isn't just a white thing

Here's a real life scenario I'll not soon forget. At a gas station recently, I pumped my car and walked to the cashier. At 5 a.m., the all-night attendant had a stern look. Then he asked, "Did you hear the gunshots last night?" He pointed across the road to a nightclub.

I shook my head.

He scrunched his face and looked me in the eye. "They were your people."

"What?"

He picked up the paper he was reading and pointed to a story of a robbery suspect killed the day before in a gunfight with police in broad daylight. Then he linked up the violence in a neat little way. "They were like him," he said. "Just like him."

I looked at the paper. The suspect was an ex-Air Force sergeant of Cambodian descent, identified as Akkadet Pathomkrut, also known as Steve Silver.

Steve Silver? The guy was a Cambodian Jew? What kind of Passover seder do they have? Whatever he was, he was Cambodian, and I am of Filipino descent. So what's with this "my people" stuff?

"What's the difference?" he asked. "You all look alike."

Ah, yes. Textbook racist comment. The phrase was not the surprising part—it's been said before. More surprising was the ethnicity of the cashier. He was an Asian Indian. Do I fight stereotype with stereotype? If I'm a violent Asian American of Filipino descent with a penchant for guns, what is he? A snake charmer? I refrained. This was my friend, my brother, after all. I've been to this gas station before, and I choose it over the one with cheaper gas across the road because I want to patronize Asian businesses.

I had been friendly with this gentleman in the past. He's an older, balder, rounder, fiftyish man from north of Delhi. In previous early morning conversations, he told me he lived in London before moving to the good old United States.

But there was no friendly chat today. Those must have been some gunshots he'd heard. He was clearly rattled.

"Filipino. Cambodian. What's the difference?" he asked again, in his slightly British Indian accent.

"I'm not Cambodian," I told him. "I'm Filipino."

"Yes, you are," he said. "And you should go back home."

"I am home," I told him. "I'm an American."

"You're not American," he said. "You are foreigner!"

I've been called a lot of things. But "foreigner?" An okay '70s rock band, but let's get our facts right. "I was born here," I said.

"No, no," he said. "You are Filipino."

"American!"

"Then wear it on your chest, American," he said pounding his heart. "You are foreigner."

"And what about you?" I asked. "You're an American?"

"I am an American," he said in his haughty tone. "For 30 years, I've been an American citizen."

What a sight. Essentially, two Asian Americans. One immigrant. One born here. Both heatedly debating just how American they are. All we needed was a white person named John Smith to walk in and put us both in our place.

No such luck. I left just before the National Guard had to be called in. Without resolution. Chalk it up to a bad night on the graveyard shift? Or was it some harbinger of future disagreement between immigrants and native born?

Last week the news came out that the immigrant population is rising. More than 25 million residents of the United States are foreign-born, nearly one-tenth of our population.

California has the largest percentage of immigrant residents with nearly 25 percent. New York has 19.6 percent. Florida, 16.4 percent; New Jersey, 15.4 percent; and Texas 11.3 percent.

Latinos make up half of the foreign born, with the greatest numbers of immigrants, seven million residents (27 percent of the foreign-born population) coming from Mexico.

Asians have the next largest numbers with the most from the Philippines (4.4 percent of the foreign born population), then China and Hong Kong with 4.3 percent.

Those numbers mean one in two immigrants speak Spanish. One in four immigrants is Asian. Just one in five is from Europe.

With the census news disseminated, I expected to hear the standard flame-throwing from the xenophobes. I heard resentment from mainstream "natives" who advocated closing the borders while we "absorb" the immigrants like a white paper towel.

But the deeper numbers show a new race front developing. One-third of foreign-born residents (about seven million people) had become citizens as of March 1997. Foreign-born Citizens (FBCs) are the New Americans.

Their stats are impressive. Unemployment was 8.4 percent for foreign-born noncitizens. But it was reduced by half, to 4.3 percent for FBCs.

And get this. That number was lower than the native-borns' unemployment rate of 5.4 percent.

The poverty rate was 26.8 percent for foreign-born noncitizens; that number was reduced by nearly two-thirds to 10.4 percent for FBCs. And that number was lower than native-borns' 12.9 percent.

What's that mean? Life is changing in the New America. For one, it's going to get harder for the xenophobes. It's no longer automatic to hate all the immigrants. It's going to be like cholesterol in diets. There's good cholesterol and bad cholesterol.

And it's not as simple as distinguishing between legal or illegal immigrants. Now it's about who has the drive and desire to be an American citizen. Judging from the poverty stats, you might say the FBCs, the foreign-born who become citizens, are clearly more desirable than those lazy good for nothing native-borns.

But my gas station experience shows that many citizen-immigrants, coming from homogenous countries, have a strange sense of tolerance in our democracy. There's a superiority. Like salmon that have made it upstream. Their perspective is more Darwin than Martin Luther King.

The sad lesson of our expanding society is that the next racist you may have to deal with most likely will be a person of color. Maybe from your own general ethnic group. People of color will outnumber whites soon. And some of them have attitudes that make the KKK seem quaint. White sheets? Any color will do in the New America.

April 16, 1998

Sticks and Stones

I**T'S NOT EASY BEING A RACIST IN AMERICA**. With all the rules and laws against it, you might say the hate business suffers a bit from over-regulation.

But as a KKK member holding a noose would say, "There are loopholes."

And just as it's hard to be a racist, it's increasingly difficult to be a good victim. For example, these days when hate involves words it's become fashionable to hide behind the First Amendment. This always puts race transgressions in a different light. It's tough when you find yourself having to tolerate people you don't like. But that's the lesson in America. And thank goodness for that. Because you may want to hide behind the First Amendment yourself someday.

The First Amendment is a handy tool. It tells us the first defense to hate speech isn't a blow to a perpetrator's windpipe. Hate speech is fought best with more speech, more words, debate, dialogue. That's the kind of talk that leads to understanding and respect.

There's one other problem with being a good victim these days. It's the racism within our ethnic communities. Asian Americans especially have been known to have a lack of tolerance for those other than our own. When we practice our own version of racial purity on the side, we lack credibility when we cry "Racism!"

Criminal Defense
How to commit a hate crime and get away with it

Hate criminals got the green light recently in a court-room in Palo Alto, California. A gigantic loop hole in the law just let a belligerent Caucasian jerk free. If you want to know how you can legally mock, ridicule, and physically beat up any member of an ethnic minority in the state of California, then read on, you salivating minority bashers you. Of course, you still can't murder anyone, but some good punching therapy can rid yourself of all those post-187/anti-affirmative action hostilities.

On the other hand, if you are a prime candidate to be beaten due to your race, ethnicity, or sexual orientation, you should definitely read on to learn how to protect yourself from both your tormentor and the law.

These insights come courtesy of the case of 19-year-old Justin Adams, now a full-time business student at Foothill College in San Mateo County. Adams, a fun-loving type, was doing what any white underachiever does during some idle time. On May 1 around 11:15 p.m., he was just hanging. In Los Altos, a tony suburb of San Francisco, he probably looked like any of the cretins on Beverly Hills 90210. He was at the local gas station, smoking cigarettes and drinking beer with three friends. He was oblivious to the world until 28-year-old Korean American John Lee entered his universe.

Lee, who's lived in California since age seven, was one tired restaurant owner looking for a little gas on his way home. According to his testimony, he was pulling away from the pumps when he saw Adams running next to the car. Adams came right up to the car, bobbing his head, palms together at mid-chest. Ah so. To Asian Americans, this is instantly recognizable as racist stunt #337, mocking a traditional sign of grace and servitude. As a bonus sound effect, Lee said the man was squinting and speaking in "Oriental gibberish." After a night in kimchee, this was the last thing restaurateur Lee needed. A white guy who thinks the world is his karaoke bar.

In court, Adams denied making fun of Lee's ethnicity. In fact, he said his actions weren't Asian specific. He had his arms folded across his chest and was highstepping. He said his head may have bobbed as a natural component of running. He could be one of those Russian guys in The Nutcracker. Or mocking a member of the "Hitler Youth Corps." He may have been squinting because he was grimacing. In any event, his body was contorted in all sorts of positions. Like comedian Jim Carrey, Adams said. Followers of the pop dance-music scene may want to dub this "The Funky Chicken defense."

With all this going on, what could Lee do? He stopped his car, rolled down the window and asked Adams what was going on. Then Lee got out of the car. Lee said he and Adams started mixing it up. Adams said Lee shoved him back three times before, in self-defense, Adams had to punch Lee in the face. For good measure, Adams punched him again.

But wait, there's more. Bruce Lee did not spontaneously re-incarnate and come to anyone's rescue but Adams' friends came charging in like the cavalry to save the endangered white man. One buddy, Ryan Keiser, tackled Lee to the ground. The other, James Calafiore, kicked Lee in the head and ribs.

Okay, you be the judge. Have I just described a hate crime? What do you suppose happened to our players here?

Keiser, the tackler, plead no contest to misdemeanor battery and was sentenced to five days in jail and 100 hours of community service. Calafiore, the kicker, plead no contest and got 45 days in jail and 200 hours of community service.

Only Adams was charged with a misdemeanor hate crime. Guess what? On Friday, Oct. 27, a jury let him go. In Palo Alto Municipal Court, the jury was deadlocked in a 10-2 vote. Only two voted to convict, the rest to acquit. When unanimity seemed hopeless, Judge Sandra Faithful declared the whole thing a mistrial.

Yes, Justin Adams has been set free.

The jurors all said they believed Justin Adams had mocked John Lee. But they said the problem was with the law. Apparently, to be guilty of a hate crime the law requires that there be threats or a threat of force. In the *San Jose Mercury News*, one juror is quoted as saying, "In the deliberations, most people felt there had been no threat of force (by Adams) to kick off the whole thing."

In other words, according to the letter of the law, to complete a transaction of a hate crime you need to have the smashing precede the slurring. "Punch, then mock." That's a sure-fire guilty. But the converse is more powerful: mocking and then punching will get you acquitted for a hate crime in California.

Is the California hate crime law inadequate? Or was it all due to poor jury instructions? That's what people are looking at now. Adams, in fact, could be retried.

In the meantime, there appears to be only one way to protect yourself legally if you're a minority. The next time you're involved in a possible hate crime, you may just want to clarify with your tormentor his or her intent. Carry a form that asks the simple question, "Does your squinting and your attempt to sound like Mickey Rooney, the Asian in *Breakfast at Tiffany's*, indicate your real intent to do physical harm to my personage?"

This will make him laugh and punch you. Or just punch you. That's when you must remember the

Tormentor's Creed: "Punch and mock convicts, mock and punch acquits."

Have him/her take a swing, and all throughout, mock him/her mocking you. This will anger your tormentor, and make him hurt you even more. Just remember, you need it for your case in court. Without it, as John Lee found out, you're in deep kimchee.

November 10, 1995

A Trio of Hate Crimes

Three recent news stories appear to be about hate crimes. In two of them, I'm ready to pounce for justice. But the third makes me question our right to complain at all.

The first story is in New York, where the Justice Department has finally begun its investigation on the beating of six Asian American and three Japanese students outside a Syracuse Denny's restaurant one early morning last month.

This apparently was not meant to be a standard part of Denny's much advertised "Grand Slam" breakfast.

In fact, the students from Syracuse University didn't even get any food at all. Upon their arrival at the restaurant, they were told they had to place their names on a waiting list. That's pretty standard. And so what if there were empty tables. Maybe the restaurant had just a few servers working that hour. But then the students noticed that groups of white males were being seated immediately.

Hmm. The sign didn't read "No shoes, No socks, No Asians."

The students complained, but to no avail. Hey, it's a

Denny's, not moot court. They were asked to leave, and found themselves escorted out by security guards, as if they were part of some "Bring Back Sambo's" conspiracy.

That's when the trouble began. According to the students' lawyers, one of the guards pushed the students, and then a "gang of about 20" white males came out shouting epithets and attacking. What were these hooligans thinking? That, indeed, the food was worth the wait? Or that there was a problem with the mere presence of foreign-looking people in, of all places, Syracuse. What stereotype fueled their rage? Because when it was over, the students' complaint filed with the Syracuse DA's office claims that two of the Asian American students were beaten unconscious.

In the complaint, one of those students, Derrick Lizardo, a Filipino American student, said: "I was never made to feel so helpless and so different in my entire life."

Two black patrons, who had also been waiting, were the only ones to come to the aid of the Asian students. Where were the security guards? The Denny's guards, off-duty sheriff's deputies, did not intervene, instead calling for police backup. By the time the police arrived, the fight was over and the attackers had left the scene.

Maybe the students should have just assumed a karate pose? Which brings us to story No. 2.

As an Asian American of Filipino descent, I know how this pose can strike fear into the hearts of thugs and bullies. I remember walking through tough neighborhoods in the '70s with my lone protection: I looked like I knew karate.

Of course I didn't. Neither did 33-year-old Kuanchung Kao, an immigrant from Taipei, an engineer and father of three. Early in the morning, Kao stood alone, outside his home in Rohnert Park, Calif. According to reports, he had gotten into an argument in a bar earlier that night.

Someone mistook him for a Japanese guy. Kao is Chinese. Then his nemesis delivered the clincher, "Well, you all look the same."

Reports indicate that Kao suddenly snapped. He had had it. When he got home, Kao was drunk. He got a stick and was doing a kind of "air warrior" thing. But he was noisy to boot, so much so that the neighbors were a bit concerned. They were trying to sleep. They called 911.

The rest is predictable. A veteran officer shows up, sees an Asian man with a stick who looks like he knows karate. Thought processes go off. Decision: Better shoot him. That's police training for you.

Forget that Kao wasn't holding anyone hostage. Nor was he a menace to anyone in particular. But the officer said he felt "threatened." After all, Kao had a stick. The officer, a gun—and a stereotypical view.

At this point, I'd be expected to go off into a rage about the stupidity of these acts perpetrated on Asians, egging on the activists who are fighting on behalf of the aggrieved.

But not so fast.

As I contemplated the two stories from both coasts, I heard the third story that stopped me dead in my tracks.

It involves a 16-year-old Oakland boy who's recovering from a shotgun blast to his back and thighs. Anthony Stamps is his name. And the suspect is described as an Asian male.

Stamps and some friends were playing with water toys and garden hoses one hot Sunday afternoon. Witnesses say a motorist became angered when some water splattered his car. Now I know water is instant death to, say, the witch in *The Wizard of Oz*. A little water on the car hardly seems to make for a shooting offense.

But tell that to the motorist. He stopped and swore at the boys. Then Stamps says the man came back with a

12- or 20-gauge shotgun. When they saw it, the boys ran. But not before 30 pieces of buckshot hit the 16-year-old, knocking him to the ground and shattering the window of a car.

Could it be that the Asian male suspect, still at large, was so anal that a little water would set him off? Or was it that proverbial last straw, this act by a black child, seen as indolent, disrespectful, and perhaps not even having a life worth living? What reaction would the man have had for an Asian with an errant squirt gun? Or a white kid in a ritzier area of Oakland?

The story exposes a fundamental problem for Asian Americans: Our community is primarily immigrant, from Asian societies that revel in their homogeneity, not to mention their penchant for racism and a lack of tolerance. More often than not, these same views are instilled in their American-born children.

It's the community's dirty little secret. Consider that many recent Asian immigrants don't even know who Martin Luther King, Jr. was. They just know he didn't speak an Asian language.

As a community, Asian Americans need to make a better effort to bridge these gaps. The fight to end anti-Asian violence rings hollow—unless we begin to curb and eliminate the racism many of us instinctively feel toward others.

May 30, 1997

'Jap' Spoken Here

Fair warning to the hypersensitive

Is it ever proper to use the word Jap? What about Flip? Or Chink? Spic? Polack? Dago? Wop? Kike? What about the champion of all racial epithets and Mark Fuhrman's favorite, nigger?

If I have left anyone out, please forgive me. I believe in equal opportunity.

I bring up these terms as a public service, to remind you that these are still just words. As such, they're merely empty symbols, letters in a demilitarized zone. That is, until they are given a context, or meaning.

That's the problem. As soon as you say any of those words you've immediately cut off any rational communication. Say the word Jap or Chink and you don't have time to explain context. You're too busy debating what you meant. Term of endearment? (Yo Nigga!) Or hate epithet? (You nigger!) And if you aren't debating vigorously, then things are just on knee-jerk autopilot. What did you say? Well of course, it's all just gutter talk. You're down with the Fuhrmans. You're talking ugly.

It ain't worth it. So most of us go amok in some other way. We don't use those words. Besides, those words are hateful, antiquated, backward. And they make people forget the First Amendment.

Case in point: Wasco, Calif. It's a town of 18,000 near Bakersfield. Levi Pagsuberon edits the town's free weekly, the *Wasco Tribune*. The 64-year-old Filipino immigrant also writes a column. Last Dec. 13, Pagsuberon got upset about what he called "Japanese hard-liners" who were denying that Japanese atrocities occurred in World War II. He also criticized a Japanese American who protested a Pearl Harbor Day celebration in which sacks of flour were dropped on placards representing Japanese war planes.

Wrote Pagsuberon: "I squirm every time I drive this Jap truck that my wife bought for me. Someday, if I have the money, I'll burn this Jap truck and buy me a Dodge Ram. And I'll really do it."

Clearly an imitator of the "Amok" style of column writing. Except for the "Jap" part. I wouldn't have been that lazy. I would have spelled out Japanese.

Pagsuberon's column caught the attention of the Los Angeles-based Media Action Network for Asian Americans (MANAA). It pointed out to the *Wasco Tribune* that Jap is no longer an acceptable abbreviation, and is considered racist. MANAA also demanded an apology.

But Pagsuberon persisted. In a Jan. 17 editorial, he defended his use of the term, saying it was directed against those Japanese who are insensitive to atrocities committed during the war.

He wrote: "It should be the Japanese who should apologize to me for the killing of many of my friends and relatives by the Japanese military during the Second World War."

MANAA, showing the utmost sensitivity in this matter, had a second-generation Filipino, Ben Bulatao, deal with Pagsuberon. It didn't work.

As Bulatao told the L.A.-based Japanese daily *Rafu Shimpo*, "It's okay to have your opinion, but the problem we have is his use of the racial slur 'Jap.' He not only hurts the people that he's targeting, but all Japanese Americans."

But Pagsuberon explained that he was just addressing his remarks "to that particular group [the Japanese Youth Liberal Party] on a specific political issue. I just did not go around calling people 'Japs.' And I did not use the word 'Jap' to a person. I said 'Jap truck.'"

Pagsuberon insisted his use of the term was a kind of slang expression. "I don't see any reason why I cannot use that word. I think people are just oversensitive," he told the *Rafu Shimpo* reporter. "We are in the United States—this is a free country."

To which Bulatao replied: "I think you have to take

responsibility for what you're going to say because of the ramifications it might have on other people. So many people try and hide behind First Amendment rights. I don't think it's that simple."

And that's where we must come to the defense of Mr. Pagsuberon. The First Amendment really is that simple. The First Amendment is for hiding.

The First Amendment protects minority opinions. It's there so that the self-righteous with occasional streaks of ignorant racism thrown in can have their say. That's America. It's there for people like Pagsuberon, too.

MANAA has been both correct and successful in getting media organizations to be more sensitive in their coverage. But MANAA would be dead wrong to go after Pagsuberon and the *Wasco Tribune* any further. MANAA can demand an apology. It can engage in dialogue. It can publicize the incident as an instructional aid. But it can't shut up Pagsuberon, can't censor his views, and can't force him to adopt MANAA's view on why Jap is a special word that requires sensitive use. If MANAA winds up empty-handed, at least there's been some public discussion.

Besides, Pagsuberon has a legitimate gripe against Japanese who are trying to sanitize their role in the Philippines and other countries during WWII. The hate, anger, and passion against the Japanese role in WWII is still very real for many Filipinos. When they say Jap they still mean it. For some reason, it's different from hearing American vets say Jap, which I abhor. The difference I think is that the U.S. won. The Philippines and its people were subjugated, treated like dirt in their own land. And the perpetrator, the Japanese government, has never fully owned up to all its actions.

The Japanese occupation of the Philippines was not pretty. My mother remembers being locked away by her parents as a young woman in Manila, for fear she would be raped. I didn't understand just how strong her feelings were until one night in San Francisco, when she absolutely refused to enter a Japanese restaurant. That was more than 30 years after the war.

And that's our problem here, folks. Older Filipinos who remember the Japanese occupation of the Philippines have a whole different context for the term Jap. It's real. It's legitimate. It still hurts. But it clashes with the current context of Jap, and any other context in which the term is hurled at Japanese Americans with hate. That's why it's just better not to use the term, or any others like it. When we don't get past a word, we don't understand each other.

February 9, 1996

Don't Shoot Schott

Even Marge is entitled to her opinions

Marge Schott owns the Cincinnati Reds, not to be confused with the Cincinnati Red Chinese. Of course, it wouldn't be the Red Chinese—that would be a state-run team. And Schott definitely isn't like the Butchers of Tiananmen. They get Most Favored Nation status. Meanwhile, Schott gets an ultimatum and a threat of muzzling. This is America, after all.

You see, Marge Schott, in her own perverse, "free-speechy" way, is like the guy who faced down the tank in Beijing that day in June 1989. The problem is, these days, everyone is saying, "Shoot her. Shoot her." This is America, after all.

But no matter what you've heard, I think it's time to come to the old bag's defense.

I don't care what she thinks of Asian Pacific Americans. I know I've said it twice before, but repetition helps. This is America, after all.

This subject comes to my attention because Marge has recently branched out. She has always had a thing for black players. She called two players who were suing her "million-dollar niggers" (November 1992). And she's had a thing for gay fashion plates. In reference to male jewelry, she's said, "Only fruits wear earrings" (May 1994).

Perhaps, her greatest hit was her statement on ESPN on May 5 when she was talking a little history for the masses, and said that Adolf Hitler was "OK at the beginning ... He just went too far."

I guess the same thing could be said for Hirohito, Marcos, Genghis Khan, and Chairman Mao. Schott didn't talk about them, which proves she knows something about restraint.

But it didn't take long for Schott to include APAs. In the May 20 issue of *Sports Illustrated*, Schott talked about Asian immigration: "Well, I don't like when they come here, honey, and stay so long and then outdo our kids. That's not right."

Only her assumption wasn't right.

For an encore, in the same interview she did her imitation of Japanese Prime Minister Kiichi Miyazawa—in her best Jerry Lewis-does-Japanese accent—"pass the buck teeth please."

Schott said: "He says to me, honey, he says, 'No want Cadirrac, no want Rincoln, want Mosh Shott Boo-ick." (Marge Schott sells used cars from her very own Buick dealership in her spare time, just in case you needed another character reference.)

OK, hold your fire on those potsticker bazookas. Reave her arone.

At press time, Marge Schott continues to stare down the barrel of the tank driven by baseball's executive committee. They have given her until my column deadline to either give up the title of chief operating officer of the team or face a suspension.

It's my hope that Big Mouth Marge has the courage to stare them down.

First of all, there's no reason to kick Schott out of baseball. If baseball owners have a complaint about how she runs her team, then maybe they have a case. If she puts more salt in the popcorn, serves hot dogs with more rat feces than other teams, leaves exposed nails in the visiting team's bench, then yeah, kick her out. But Schott runs her team effectively. The Reds have the second highest payroll in baseball, with $40,719,334 paid to employees. Despite sub-par efforts from key players this year, the team is still competitive in baseball's weakest division. Kick Marge out?

Okay, so what about her words? She speaks her personal thoughts not as an owner of the team, but as a private citizen. Isn't someone entitled to an opinion around here?

But Emil, this woman is a racist, a bigot. She's a walking hate crime!

Well, not so fast ye of high sensitivity. We've got this thing here called the Bill of Rights.

It's more important than your utility bill. And it has this beauty of a thing called the First Amendment. It protects unpopular, even stupid opinions from being stifled. America, land of free enterprise, is the free market of ideas, where debate supposedly flourishes. Words are like your favorite ball players: free agents. But remember it's subject to competition. So all views must fend off challenges. The public witnesses the exchange of ideas, and usually sides with the most logical, most compelling ones.

Censure Marge Schott? Stifle her comments? What for? Has she done anything illegal? No. Her comments are nothing but a rube's babble. Marge Schott's opinions are harmless. Debate her all you want. You'd massacre her. You can defeat her with both hands tied behind your back.

But get angry and lift a finger to shut her up, punish her in some way, and suddenly you've crossed the line. And there you are standing with the Butchers of Beijing.

Oh sure, there's nothing wrong with Schott that a few dabs of Super Glue applied to her Mary Kay lipstick couldn't fix. But that would be like putting a cat in a microwave to test for internal combustion. Inhumane. Undemocratic.

Marge Schott, famous for wearing clothes that make Kathie Lee Gifford's Honduran fashions look haute couture, has been vilified because she does not walk softly and carry a big stick. She talks loudly and sticks foot in mouth. Often.

So, should she be shown out of town in a runaway rickshaw? Should she be muzzled like a dog, and sent to her room without food? Should she be pilloried in the media and left for dead, with flies circling the carrion?

No.

We've had our fun; let's leave her alone.

Marge Schott is a doddering fool.

Kicked out of baseball? Hey, GM doesn't kick her out of the car business. And besides, we're supposed to be bigger than any bigots.

So I'm reaching out to Marge. I want to help. Maybe she doesn't see enough APAs in Cincinnati. If that's the case, I would "sentence" her to co-hosting with Martin Yan, of *Yan Can Cook* fame. Yan could show her the versatility of his accent. Marge could show Yan how to cook with beer.They can even compare regional sausages.

That should do it. But I'm warning her. If she offers to cook her dog on the show, that's it.

Of course, all bets are off if Marge backs down to baseball. If she quits and gives in, there won't be any special rehab for her. And I, for one, will be sorely disappointed. But then courage is the last thing one expects from a bigot.

June 14, 1996

Isn't That Hysterical!
Why a racist magazine cover isn't all bad

Flash! There's an Asian American in the White House. And he's not a guest in the Lincoln Bedroom, either. He's the president of the United States. Asian Americans across the country are outraged! In fact, this may be our community's great test. Can we keep it up?

All of it is courtesy of the *National Review*, that aging right wing publication doing its darnedest to get noticed these days. Not since the John Birch Society has the *National Review* managed to raise anyone's dander. Short of a cover featuring Clarence Thomas in Dennis Rodman drag, what else can a desperate rag do? Go racist, of course.

So with its aim on the Asian Campaign Donation Controversy, what I call the Asian American community's ACDC problem, the recent *National Review* cover depicts Al Gore in a monk's robe. (Insert guffaw here.) Nothing too wrong there. He did attend a fundraiser at a Buddhist temple, after all.

Then there's Hillary, dressed in a Mao suit clutching a little red book. Or was that her health-care primer?

(Insert knee slap here. Boy, that modern satire is a killer!) Just for good measure, the magazine gives the first lady slanted eyes and huge buck teeth the size of the Oval Office.

The president's treatment is even more colorful, shall we say. Clinton dons a Chinese coolie hat held down on his head by a taut string wrapped around a bulbous nose. He's serving up some hot tea on a tray for whoever has a contribution. Point made. But once again, the magazine goes for its ethnic topper: Baggy eyes, squinty and sloped, and buck teeth fitting for a president who'd do anything for a fundraiser. The man from Hope gets an oversized set of narrow teeth that leaves his lips pursed in such a way that you can almost hear him utter the syllables, "ah-so."

The president, vice president, and first lady are taking so much foreign campaign money, they're turning Asian! But does the punchline hit below the belt? Has the *National Review*'s stab with its rubber sword become one of the most overt examples of public racism since the days of "Darkie" toothpaste and "Sambo's?"

In an interview, Editor John O'Sullivan defended his cover: "Caricature in the very nature of things, deals to some extent in stereotypes. If this were a scandal involving Russians, they'd be shown with snow on their boots and wearing fur hats."

But putting on a set of strange garments is one thing. Giving the president and first lady slanted eyes and buck teeth crosses the line. By O'Sullivan's standards, with the first lady visiting Africa, would he dare a cover featuring Hillary carrying a spear and a plate in her mouth? America would recognize foul play immediately.

Asian Americans have demanded an apology. "We fully appreciate artistic license and recognize that caricatures are often used to lampoon political figures," Asian

American leaders said in a statement issued last week through the Congressional Asian Pacific American Caucus Institute. "What we do not appreciate is the *National Review*'s shameless abuse of its so-called artistic license to propagate a flagrantly racist depiction."

Ironically, O'Sullivan, the culprit, has taken on the stature of aggrieved victim. He's mustered the gall to refer to the charges of racism against his magazine as "vile and slanderous, the result of an orchestrated campaign by the Ethnic Grievance Industry."

There's an immigrant in need of a reality check.

But maybe I needed one too.

As an Asian American who often uses satire, I like the First Amendment as much as the next guy. But there was something smelly about this *National Review* cover. I would have exaggerated Clinton's traits, or given them all money bags. But to give Bill and Hillary features stereotypically Asian? That requires a choice that goes beyond satire. It's racist.

So as not to be accused of being either "politically correct" or "overly sensitive," I did the only thing the O'Sullivans of the world could respect. I sought out the opinion of a white man. And boy do I feel better. Nothing like white validation.

Guess what? He was offended too.

"The teeth more than anything else are almost a signature of a racist anti-Asian cartoon," said Bob Callahan, a Berkeley resident and the author of *The Big Book of American Irish Culture*. "There's a history of manipulating the bodies of minority people to show they are less than human, or infantile, or diseased. That's what's going on here."

Callahan said it's like the Irish being depicted as monkeys by old British newspapers. Irish people know it as a kind of hate code. Asian Americans are the same with buck teeth and slanted eyes. "I imagine Asian people never saw that kind of image without getting a kind of chill," Callahan said. "Because they knew the people doing it were racist."

I started taking the cover around to my friends to see what they thought. Very few laughed. No one mentioned the First Amendment.

Callahan says it's not just Asian Americans who should be upset. But all people. "It's not so much standing up for Asian Americans," he told me. "It's about recognizing that a consensus does exist, and that there is a standard that all Americans can rely on that assures that their individual heritage can be respected."

Ultimately that's what it's all about: a standard of fair play. It's lacking in the *National Review* cover. A week after the issue has been released, Asian Americans aren't giving up their demand for an apology. And they shouldn't. When racist images go unchallenged, they become part of the culture.

That's what makes the cover issue a true test of the community's strength. Ever since the ACDC issue surfaced, I've been monitoring the egregious examples of racist coverage in the media. There was the darkened black and white cover photo of the "sinister" James Riady in *Newsweek*, so reminiscent of the darkened O.J. Simpson *Time* magazine cover. Then William Safire's hysterical speculation that Chinese spies have been funneling money to U.S. campaigns based on his own recollection of a great Chinese spy. Seen one, seen them all. Now this.

Only two outcomes seem possible. With the upcoming hearings in Washington, the *National Review* cover could be the harbinger of a form of acceptable racism toward Asian Americans. "Charlie Chan Days" are back in America. Hey, everybody let's do the new hip-hop rage, the "Coolie."

Or this racist cover thing could be exactly what we need to strengthen our Pan Asian community's sense of political resolve.

April 4, 1997

Apologists for Powell
So what's wrong with 'Chinamen'?

Earlier this year I was banging a gong for Colin Powell. The idea of a person of color who could actually be President of the United States was as tantalizing as it gets on the presidential dim sum cart. Dole? err. Clinton? hmm. But Powell, ahh... So, he sounded like the perfect Asian American candidate. Overachieving, traditionally conservative on family and economic issues. Progressive on race. Pro-affirmative action. Ultimately, he didn't run, but so what? He was "The Great Person of Color's Hope."

Then at a speech in Stockton, Powell revealed his soul: "If you give 1.3 billion Chinamen access to home shopping on television, [communism] is over because there is no way communism can compete with a salad shooter for $9.95."

Actually, in a communist society, everyone wouldn't need salad shooters, except for the elite, who would have several per household.

But I digress.

The key word in the Powell speech is of course, not "salad shooter," nor "communism." It isn't even "home shopping," which frankly, after shipping and handling would have a hard time selling its cheap zircons against stiff competition from lowballing jewelers and trinket sellers in any Chinatown. No, the key word in the Powell speech is "Chinamen."

This is not a word that would appear on the SATs. This is not a word that one would use to be a big hit among Asian Americans. Yet here was Powell, at a talk on affirmative action and the global economy to business leaders. I guess he was just trying to show how hip he was for a with-it black man.

Since the speech, Powell has apologized.

In a letter Wednesday to the Organization of Chinese Americans and the Japanese American Citizens League, Powell said the reference was inappropriate and he would never use it again.

"I apologize for any offense [my remarks] may have caused to any member of the Chinese and Pacific American communities."

But he also tried to defend it a little bit.

"The context in which I used the word was a positive one as I recounted the economic progress being made in China by the unleashing of the creative and entrepreneurial potential of the Chinese people," the letter said.

With all due respect, that's a pretty weak excuse. Saddam Hussein would be all over his face on that one. Powell may point out economic progress on one hand, but it's negated by the use of an image—the Chinaman slave, the exploited laborer who came to America to build a railroad and settle the West.

The fact that Powell is now doing coolie work for Dole doesn't help him in my eyes either. You can say he's taken a drop in my poll.

End of story?

Well, no.

First, there were a surprising number of Powell apologists.

Diana Griego Erwin, the lovely and talented columnist

for the *Sacramento Bee*, wrote a piece titled, "Powell Didn't Mean Disrespect."

She writes: "Was Powell's remark insensitive, viewed through the clear lens of retrospect? Yes. Were some Chinese Americans offended? Sure. Should Powell have known better? Of course."

Okay, so far so good. But here's where she turns into an apologist.

"But then you must ask whether [Powell] aimed to disrespect, wound, or disparage the Chinese or Americans of Chinese ancestry. The answer, anyone looking at Powell's record, would say, is absolutely not. How ludicrous."

Not too ludicrous. He's a politician. They say one thing and do another. This was no "slip" of the tongue. His speech was a prepared, premeditated act. Could it happen to the best of us? Sure. But most of us didn't head up the Joint Chiefs, nor consider running for president. To say he didn't mean to offend isn't good enough. Okay, so he isn't insensitive and malicious, he's just ignorant.

Besides, who cares about Powell? What about the aggrieved? If Asian Americans are hurt, then who is Powell, who is anyone to deny that we aren't? Even if it were an unintentional slur, an accident, does that make a difference? Say it was actually a gun shot, accidental, that hit us squarely, can Powell, can anyone stand by our wound and convince us that we don't hurt?

Second, since the remark, I can't tell you how many times people have asked me "What's wrong with 'Chinaman'?"

This is a problem.

A few older Asian Americans called me on my talk show heard in Northern California, and were quite surprised it was even an issue. They cited context. "It's not a big deal," they said. But certainly it was a big deal. I asked them why Powell couldn't use the term "Chinese." To say "Chinamen" is derogatory and sexist. It's a slur. It gets in the way of communication. Furthermore, it's a real choice. When you greet a female, you wouldn't use the term "bitch." Not even if she were your dog.

A white male friend who was upset over the issue complained that if he couldn't use the word, no one should. This white guy gets upset when hip blacks call each other "nigger." So in order to eradicate "Chinamen" from his vocabulary he is requesting that Asians refrain from referring to themselves in lovingly self-deprecating phrases such as, "Yo, Chinaman!"

While we're at it, and since turnabout is fair play, I am seeking the eradication of a few potentially volatile phrases:

"Nip in the air." Just say, "It's cold."

"Flip phone." Cell phone will do.

And since there were no Chinese in King Arthur's Court, we shall seek elimination of the phrase, "Chink in the armor." This month, Gen. Powell showed he had a major one in his.

October 18, 1996

The Price of Racism
$300,000 settles a housing discrimination suit

If you've ever wanted to sue for discrimination on the basis of race, a recent case involving five Stanford students is instructive. True justice is hard to come by, even if you have the winning hand.

First of all, it's tough to prove discrimination in a court of law. It's almost easier to prove Saddam Hussein has weapons of mass destruction.

53

But for either, it seems you just about have to go to war.

The scale of such interventions is, of course, relative. Still, war is war, and if engaged, you grit your teeth, vow you'll never give up, and press on to victory. It's the only way to fight. That is, until you get to the point that everyone says, "Hey, we have lives to live. Let's settle this thing."

People involved in discrimination suits tend to reach that point a whole lot faster than Saddam Hussein.

That would about sum up the situation for Teri Chew, Kim Chiu, Carrie Tzou, Dianne Chen, and Lori Sakoda, five Asian American Stanford women. A few years ago they were roommates looking for a nice off-campus place to rent and call home.

Their house hunt turned ugly when they toured a home owned by Janette Hybl in Menlo Park, Calif.

In August 1996, the quintet filed a lawsuit against Hybl in federal court in Oakland alleging violations of federal and state fair housing laws and civil hate crime laws.

The suit claimed that after showing them the house, Hybl told the women that she already had "good, white American applicants."

Oh-oh. Do I hear a "Bingo?"

In passing, Hybl also reportedly told the women that "you people are ruining this country," and that "white people need to stick together."

For a grand finale, while the students stood in the driveway of the home trying to figure out what had just transpired, Hybl reportedly came back out, chased the women from her property, shook her fists and yelled, "Go back to your country."

Of course, they were already here.

Considering the rhetoric, it would seem that the girls

have a slam dunk case. And what punishment would be suitable for someone like Hybl? To be hung by the thumbs over a bowl of won ton soup? To be placed in a cell and forced to watch Chinese language television programming without subtitles? Ha!

Of course, justice doesn't work that way. It's never that satisfying.

First of all, the culprits always have an answer. In a deposition, Janette Hybl tried the tactic often used by former and current presidents. She testified to having no recollection of any of the events recalled by the women. In fact, Hybl and her parents, the owners of the property, denied any liability whatsoever.

The judge in the case, however, found differently and issued an order finding the defendants liable for violations of the fair housing laws and the civil hate crime statute. At that point, people started to take the proceedings a whole lot more seriously. An offer to settle was made, and everyone accepted. Justice achieved, right?

Sort of.

The girls got money. The Hybls saved face.

The five girls received $300,000—total.

The Hybls agreed to refrain from violating federal and state fair housing laws and to take some sensitivity-type training on how to obey the law. Great. But don't all good citizens already tacitly agree to refrain from violating any federal and state laws? What was gained here? Most importantly, the Hybls got off without having to admit to any liability at all. Essentially, what they ended up doing was paying for the Stanford girls' tuition. And as for the housing discrimination issue, officially, the Hybls did nothing wrong. They're clear. Their wallets are lighter, but they probably had some insurance company cover the settlement.

Said Marcel Hawiger, executive director of Midpeninsula Citizens for Fair Housing: "Even though money doesn't erase the emotional injury, it's certainly compensation, and hopefully it will send a signal that race discrimination is illegal and hurtful."

His key phrase: "Even though money doesn't erase the emotional injury ... " It sure doesn't. What, after all is the price of racism? Were the landlord's slurs worth $60,000 a student? Or much more? I know that if I sue, my goal wouldn't be money. It would be to bring people to justice. Throwing money at me doesn't make me whole. If it's all about race and not about class, then forget the money. If you make me whole with money, what does that say? Money makes me equal?

So what's the best remedy? It's not necessarily a big payday. In fact, I'd rather see a racist grovel at my feet. Now that's priceless.

But what happens in this case? The students get bought off with a compromise, a full and final settlement. They go from being victims of racism to beneficiaries of racism. Is that vindication enough when the racists get away without admitting the deed?

Hawiger said that "hopefully" this case may send a signal. Who's he kidding. Yeah, here's the signal to racists everywhere: Like anything else in America, with a little cash, you can get away with anything. Even discrimination. That's what is so unsettling about settling. It ain't justice. But for our system, all too often it's considered good enough.

February 17, 1998

Addicted to Equal Opportunity

I can't help it. I like the high I get when I stand tall and am recognized for my talents. Affirmative action programs did that for me. More than being "qualified," I was visible.

But now, we've destroyed it.

It used to be that people who were historically under-represented, overlooked, and denied access to institutions had legitimate claims to openings for jobs and education. We were fighting discrimination.

Affirmative action was our tool and the best programs always worked on both sides. Society had a chance to rectify its failure; I had a chance to affirm my excellence.

Now the definition of affirmative action has changed so that whites who are generally more represented, more visible, and have greater total access to employment and education can be assured that they maintain a piece of the action. They're not fighting discrimination. They're fighting competition from qualified minorities. And they're doing it by an "affirmative action" of their own. It's called "preserving market share."

Affirmative action was strong medicine for an illness that's still there, and getting worse. But now we've thrown out the good medicine. We're letting the illness fester. And no one seems to want to lift a finger.

Life with Prop. 209

How to beat the affirmative action addiction

"**H**i. My name is Emil G. and I'm an affirmative action slut."

"Slut?" It's true. I never met an affirmative action program I didn't like. I loved them all. They gave me, a qualified person of color, a chance to show my stuff.

I came up with my "slut" analogy two years ago after a damaging Supreme Court decision declared federal efforts to expand opportunities for minorities unconstitutional.

In that decision, Judge Clarence Thomas wrote, "Government cannot make us equal ... These programs stamp minorities with a badge of inferiority and may cause them to develop dependencies or to adopt an attitude that they are entitled to preferences."

Ah, I get it. It was my problem. Yes, I was a user. I got track marks up and down my arm. I was even hooked on the big "H"—Harvard.

Back in 1995 I was just joking about my dependence on affirmative action and the idea of starting a new AA: Affirmative Action Anonymous. The AA-A. I figured that certainly, people would see through Thomas' illogical conclusion. Government can make us equal when opportunity is denied. "Stamp of inferiority?" Affirmative action gave me a chance to compete.

But now that the Supreme Court has refused to hear the case to overturn Proposition 209, it's clear we need my new AA-A more than ever.

These last two years, I had hoped the forces of good would prevail in the courts. Instead, opponents of affirmative action found ways to confuse the issue of fairness and equality by disguising the rhetoric. Prop. 209 is an ingeniously written piece of bile made to look like angel food cake. "Civil Rights Initiative" sounds good. The reality is anything but. The statistics from the University of California law schools, where a "color-blind" admissions policy was passed a year before 209, show catastrophic results. Just one black entered UC Berkeley's Boalt Hall this year. At the University of California, Los Angeles, law school, there are 50 blacks and Latinos enrolled in the first year class—the lowest numbers since affirmative action began in 1967. Re-segregation is upon us.

Asian Americans, in general, have fared far better. Enrollment at UCLA Law jumped by 70 percent. But there's no joy among Filipinos, the largest Asian minority in the state. Excluded from targeted programs for some time, Filipinos are nearly invisible throughout the UC system.

Clearly, colorblind policies and 209 are not the way to ensure equality at this time. But 209 never seemed to be about answers—just political vengeance. The only thing 209 ever addressed is the abolition of the existing remedy. And though the remedy worked, 54 percent of the voters said they didn't like an "affirmative action" that called for "preferential treatment."

So where are the answers to diversity and equality? In that regard, 209 is bankrupt. It codified the ideal and de-codified the recipients. Race, gender? This new law is for everyone. Especially white people. No wonder it's gaining momentum throughout the country. And what happens when a large number of states decide to conflict with federal civil rights law? Anyone want to revisit that states' rights debate? Anyone want to fight a new civil war?

What to do? People can continue to cry about affirmative action. They can even root for future legal challenges, but the sad fact is the majority of legal challenges will now come from whites claiming discrimination.

Lawyers will fight it out, no doubt. But how many years are you willing to wait for action? There's a reason people get put on the Supreme Court for life. More often than not, that's how long the legal process takes. For the rest of us, we better get out of our affirmative action funk and start looking for "affirmative solutions."

Several recent ideas, mostly related to education, offer some hope. Last month, Education Secretary Richard Riley said that math was the great equalizer. Students exposed to higher level math were achievers, regardless of family income or public or private schooling. For example, 83 percent of all students who took algebra and geometry went to college. Not only that, once in the work force they earned 38 percent more per hour than students without exposure to higher math.

We're not talking calculus. Just algebra and geometry. Solve for x. Pythagorean theory stuff.

But here's the rub. Only 25 percent of U.S. eighth graders are enrolled in algebra, and low-income and minority students are even less likely to take it.

Does offering math to our kids sound like one affirmative solution?

Here's another one: Delaine Eastin, California's Superintendent of Public Instruction, has proposed a plan to make the state guarantee free public education to preschool-age children starting at age four. Studies show that in areas like Los Angeles, wealthy kids are twice as likely as poor or middle class kids to attend preschool. A public preschool program could help address educational inequity from the very beginning.

These are just two ideas. We'll need more. For example, solutions to fight workplace discrimination will take a major social revolution. We may be in the midst of it. On the television program I host, *NCM: New California*

Media, demographer David Hayes-Bautista of UCLA pointed out that inter-racial dating among teenagers shows an acceptance of a multi-racial America. These young whipper snappers may not know who Martin Luther King, Jr. was, but they have discovered a love for one another that may change society.

These are all "affirmative solutions" happening right now. But the only way to recognize them is by leaving the legal morass of affirmative action to the lawyers. Let them fight in court. While we wait for logic to prevail, the rest of us should fight for more immediate, practical remedies.

Just remember we won't find real solutions until we admit to our "need." I know it's tough saying good-bye to good ole' affirmative action. But, politically it's dead. For now. So go cold turkey, join AA-A. Whenever you feel the pang of racism upon you, join me in this little prayer: "Forgive me, higher power, I'm dependent on fairness and equal opportunity." Say that little prayer. Count to 10. If it still feels bad, then sue.

November 6, 1997

Anonymously Yours

Is name-blind admissions race censorship?

The University of California's graduate admissions process will be race-blind starting in the fall. But that's not enough for Regent Ward Connerly. The man who sold the state on its "would-be colorblindedness" through Proposition 209 is now pushing for a name-blind policy. In fact, in an increasingly multicultural and diverse world, it's an absurd notion. Connerly is pushing for a new de-ethnicized California, where race is a dirty word. He's advocating for race censorship.

Said Connerly in a published report: "If you have a culture of resistance, which we have at many of our campuses, where people are going to defy the will of the regents, we're well-advised to eliminate that one overriding indicator of a person's ethnicity, and that's the name."

If Connerly wants control over administrators who are part of a "culture of resistance," there are ways to deal with that without messing around with the admissions process. He can always find new admissions officers from among his cronies. But Connerly's suspicion should come as no surprise. He's like the admissions officers of the past who felt affirmative action was rammed down their throats and did all they could to debase its fair and proper implementation. Now that the shoe's on the other foot, their suspicion is totally understandable. In fact, Connerly's proposal is an admission of just how subjective, and perhaps racist, the admissions process has been all along.

But let's say Connerly is right on the mark. Names are "ethnic tip-offs." Really? What can you tell about a name? They're loaded with individual histories and highly misleading.

Take Connerly's name. Ward isn't Jamaal, Hernando, or my favorite Filipino name, Bong Bong. Nope, the name is "Ward Connerly." A safe name. Maybe a white name. The only Ward I know of, besides the one in a hospital, would be one named Cleaver. Beaver's dad. The Cleavers were the epitome of white America. But to many African Americans, another set of Cleavers were the epitome of Black Power. As for the surname Connerly, it sounds Irish, but to say Connerly himself is Irish would be a stretch. Even during the week we celebrate St. Patrick's Day.

If turnabout is fair play, let's examine my name: Emil

Guillermo.

Spanish, right? Mexican, perhaps. Maybe Salvadoran, since I'm from the Mission. But wait. What about that first name. Could I be German? Maybe French?

Nope. Emil is not Emile. It's short for Emiliano. So I have no blood lines to the Kaisers or to Louis (pick a number). The surname may be Spanish, but I'm not Latino. History's imperial forces have given me a Spanish last name, but geography makes me Asian, more precisely Filipino. My parents' immigration makes me Filipino American. All of that is a part of my history. More than 1.5 million Filipino Americans in the United States, many with Spanish surnames, have a story like mine.

In fact, all people have a similar tale to tell about their names. They're interesting, unique parts of ourselves. They are not necessarily the dead giveaways to an over- or under-represented class. Names are deceptive. They shouldn't be a decisive part of an application. They only identify an individual. What's to fear?

"If you believe Berkeley has too many Asians and you see the name Suzie Wong, then you believe Suzie Wong might be in the over-represented class," Connerly told a reporter.

It's unfortunate that Connerly used a name known by many as the name of an Asian prostitute in a 1960 film. He could have used Connie Chung. But by his name logic, would Connerly identify the Confederate general, Robert E. Lee, as the finest Asian American military tactician?

Connerly is like an anal retentive in a Silicon Valley clean room. He wants to eradicate any evidence of cultural history that may spoil his de-ethnicized vision. But the name thing just doesn't work. If you take off the name, why not just take out all indicators of race.

That's the kind of policy that would have Connerly in

hog heaven. Consider the ideal Connerly admissions application, with the all-important student essay that would read:

"I'm (censored). I'm from (censored).

"My extra-curricular time has been spent in cultural activities like the (censored) club, the (censored) club, and the (censored) club. I learned a lot about myself as a (censored). Especially, the history of my parents from (censored). In fact, I learned enough to do a term paper in (censored) immigration to this country.

"My parents are proud that I'm applying to UC. It's a wonderful university that takes pride in diversity and in fairness to all people, especially (censored). I especially like your (censored) studies department."

It's no longer a college application. It's more like a document from J. Edgar Hoover's file. Race becomes the new classified information. Want to know my race? File a Freedom of Information Act form.

Worse yet is the prospect of the face-to-face interviews, mandatory for UC's medical schools. What would Connerly suggest? A standard-issue body bag with a little speaking hole? And then what about accents? Maybe the interviewee can pass back little notes? Or have a real-live cyberchat?

What's an admissions officer to tell from any of that? The only thing of importance becomes the bottom line: test scores. Grades. And then we run the risk of having student bodies that are so out-of-whack, they don't reflect the true diversity and greatness of our state.

We end up with the same problem we were trying to eradicate when diversity became the motto on campus: homogenized, exclusive academic communities.

But besides creating an almost impossible and unnatural admissions situation, Connerly is really exemplifying the attitude of what I call California's

"New Paranoid." Taking colorblindedness to the nth degree only indicates that Connerly must be scared that we will truly discover exactly who we are, and where we are in history. It's the ultimate denial. Eliminating race from our identity won't change the multicultural direction of our society. You can't replace racism with race censorship.

March 21, 1997

Race Matters

PEOPLE ASK ME, "Why is it that blacks and Asians can't get along?" Korean grocers have had a hell of a time in black neighborhoods on the East Coast. It was even worse in Los Angeles where Koreans in South Central Los Angeles were seen as vigilante heroes during the Los Angeles riots. More often than not, their targets were African American.

In trying to understand the phenomenon, a good first step is understanding the cultural tendencies that create "acceptable" racist attitudes. Add to that a mix of American attitudes, and some Asians are less likely to see eye to eye with blacks. When it comes to race matters, you'll find a lot of Asians who think they're white.

In big "race stories" of the day, most people are still hung up on the Black/White paradigm to even notice that Asians aren't even in the picture. Few stories ever get beyond "skin deep."

So when stories break like the O.J. case, the Sprewell/Carlesimo fight, or the Clinton Race Initiative, I always look for the Asian American link. Some may say it's a stretch. But a connection is almost always there. It's just not what we might presume it to be. And that's what makes it all the more revealing about Asian Americans.

But you'll only discover it through frank and honest discussions on race.

Skin Deep

Just between us Flips

O.J. Simpson got justice. He had the money to fight for it. That was plain to me. But apparently not too many I've bumped into in the Asian American community think justice was served.

The week after the trial of the century, I attended a typical Asian-style gathering. Family and close friends hovered around a buffet of a thousand dishes. With a big paper plate full of food, we all engaged in small talk, which this week was a one-note, two-letter exercise. O.J.

"He's guilty," said one woman, whom I didn't recognized, but assumed was an aunt of some sort. Actually, she was related to my cousin by way of marriage. Whatever she was, she ate like a relative. A well-groomed woman in her 50s, she was a recent immigrant from the Philippines who spoke with a slight accent. She seemed intelligent, until she opened her mouth. "He's geelty as seen," she said.

"The jury said not guilty," I protested. At that point, I suddenly realized this was probably not the best thing to do while standing in front of a table adorned by the head of a roast pig, and that Filipino delicacy known as dinaguan, cut up pork in a tangy black sauce. Known euphemistically as "chocolate meat," in actuality, it is merely bits of dead animal cooked in its own blood.

With entrees like that, who needs tasteful dinner conversation? But this woman was just getting revved up. "That jury was so stupid!" she said. "We need smart ones. Professional ones."

Oh, that's a great idea. Professional jurors can be ranked just like ball players. We'll have statistics on them, showing how often they vote to convict. That way attorneys could select them like they draft expansion ball players. Conviction rates would read like batting averages. In this law and order world, you'd want at least someone who batted a 1000. Now that's all-star justice for you. Even a former athlete like O.J. could get into those stats.

I was just about to launch into a "professional jury is more stupid than you are lady" diatribe when the woman shifted gears and caught me totally by surprise. Perhaps she was just feeling comfortable that we were all members of the same extended family. Whatever her reason, she seemed right at home with her emotions. In no uncertain terms, she said plainly: "You know Fuhrman was probably right. What's wrong with those tapes? O.J. is a nigger. He did it."

I nearly dropped my food. There was no "wink-wink, just us Flips here" disclaimer. Not even a "Shh, just between you and me and the coconut tree" kind of preface. From an unmarried woman like her, I would have expected to hear about the 911 call, or the battering of Nicole. But she went straight for the social jugular. This wasn't a slip. It was as if she had become emboldened by the O.J. verdict to let her raw feelings known.

I just wanted to get away from her. There is nothing attractive about a racist eating pig's blood. But I didn't want to make a scene at my cousin's party. At least that was my excuse. Then, I looked around me, and it was as if nothing had been said. They all just kept staring at the pig blood in their party plates.

Finally someone entered the room, and the talk switched to the typical family party fare. Anything but the racism that was as obvious to me as the mushrooms in the pan-fried noodles.

Now of course you, dear reader, are not a racist. But I would bet my last hunk of tofu that scene was played out in the majority of Asian American homes in our nation.

Truth be told, Asian Americans have lots of problems with race. It's just rarely acknowledged. We don't want to talk about it. There's always a better time (later), or a better place (somewhere else). In fact, we're better off not talking about it. Or being dishonest about it, so as not to offend. It's socially acceptable to hide behind such white lies in America.

Asian American racism shouldn't be such a shocking concept. Our countries of origin are predominantly homogenous. China and Japan may have individual provincial, nationalistic, and ideological struggles. They can hate each other or themselves on substantial issues. At least everyone looks alike. Perhaps in a diverse country, such as the Philippines, with all its many conquerors, you'd find an Asian sense of race harmony. Sadly, even in the Philippines race tolerance is a foreign notion. Just ask the light skinned Euro-Christian Filipinos in the rich sections of Manila how they feel about the darker-skinned Moslems in the southern part of the country. Or ask what people on the street think of the Chinese-Filipinos. It would probably be unprintable.

No wonder Asians have such a hard time with diversity when they come to America. Racial domination is more their style. Harmony is as alien to them as singing the Star Spangled Banner.

To American-born Asians, the "Asian in a strange land" idea would explain our parents' Archie Bunker tendencies. We can intellectualize the ignorance of our forefathers. But that can't be miskaken for progress. At present new immigrants make up nearly 70 percent of the Asian Pacific American community. Generations of born-here's are outnumbered. The community is an imported one. Not homegrown. As the community grows, American-borns can see and hear our parents' views replicated. Old attitudes immediately recognized as ignorant and racist are new again, mouthed in a new era of race volatility by a new wave of immigrants.

And it goes beyond O.J. Before the dinner party ended, the racist woman walked by me wanting to dish out more. "You know that Powell guy?" she asked. "I'd never vote for that man to be President. He's a black guy too." Once again a birthday party is hardly a place to open a discussion on that topic. Unless it was Martin Luther King's birthday. I passed.

It's been said that the O.J. trial has forced America to deal with the issue of race, and that the good of the trial will be all the open conversations of race throughout society.

Instead of looking away and avoiding those discussions, we better start having them soon. Until they happen in the Asian American community, the most startling revelation of the O.J. trial to me has been this: Asian Americans have more in common with Mark Fuhrman than any of us think.

October 13, 1995

Foot-Binding Book Lists

S.F. schools miss the point: Great books transcend race

I remember reading Pearl Buck's *The Good Earth* in one of my English literature classes in the San Francisco public schools in the 1960s. The classic tale of an American's view of China probably wouldn't be taught today. Ms. Buck, a great writer, would be drummed out as being "politically incorrect," or more politely, considered tragically out of style. I could see an administrator discarding volumes of Pearl Buck, in

71

favor of, say, the more contemporary Amy Tan. What a mistake that would be.

Though Ms. Buck is white, I remember the book as well-written and enjoyable, even if it was assigned. And I recall being extremely fascinated by references to foot-binding, that cultural tradition of tying up women's feet to keep them small, pretty, and ineffective. After years, that's the one thing that stands out—my classmates reaction to foot-binding. *EEEeeeek*. It made my tight pants (the style of that day) seem comfortable.

But that's what came to mind when I heard of the proposal in the San Francisco public schools that would require 40 percent of books read by students to come from ethnic minority authors. Such a rigid rule is as unnatural as foot-binding, or at least tight pants. Whatever your fancy, it's hardly the right solution to address the very real issue of diversity.

By the way, I use the term "minority" with some reservation. As we know from demographers, 2050 is the projected date the nation's minorities become the majority. In California, that date is closer to 2015. And in some areas of California, we're already there. In the world of the San Francisco public schools—64,000 students strong—nearly 90 percent of the students are from ethnic "minorities." Sounds like a majority to me.

So here's the problem: What do you teach a school district where 90 percent of the people have nothing in common, at least on the surface, with Jane Austen, Emily Bronte, or William Shakespeare? How do you make things real?

The answer, says Steve Phillips, a member of the San Francisco School Board, is to have this multicultural group of students read more books by people of color. Initially, Phillips wanted seven of 10 books. A board colleague, Keith Jackson, even suggested that five of the 10 be from black authors, even though blacks make up less than 15 percent of the high school population. Asian Americans make up 42 percent. Who's advocating for authors like Frank Chin?

Finally, the pair has loosened the foot-bind, and say they'll settle for four out of 10 books. Expanding the number of books teachers can choose from is a much better alternative. But a quota?

"Students tell me they know other kids who have dropped out because they felt the curriculum was too alienating," Phillips told a reporter. "Our curriculum needs to speak to the realities of our time."

So when do Coolio, Puff Daddy, or Snoop Doggy Dog get invited to do a teaching stint?

Phillips and Jackson seem so misguided on this. It's like they should be on the front lines of the ethnic studies debates of the 1960s. We won that one already.

If kids are dropping out of school, it's not because they were alienated and couldn't connect with *Wuthering Heights*. Now there's a story of class and alienation. What do you mean a kid from the inner city can't relate to Heathcliff? Don't blame the books. Most students probably weren't good enough readers to tackle them by the time they got to high school. What was their preparation? How were they taught in elementary school?

And let's not just blame the students. They bear a responsibility, but so do the teachers. With multiple classes, multiple problems, who has the patience or inclination to teach *Wuthering Heights* anymore?

If Phillips and Jackson want more than a lukewarm revisiting of the multicultural debate, they ought to look at the real problems. It's not the books. It's the humans—the students and teachers.

Prepare the students from first grade. Hire teachers in the schools who know how to teach a diverse, multicultural student population. Leave the books alone.

I say this with some authority, being a proud successful graduate of the San Francisco public schools, a Filipino kid on the school lunch program who got into Harvard.

I grew up in the Haight and was taught phonics in first grade at Andrew Jackson. We moved to the Mission for second grade where I attended Edison (now viewed as a "troubled" school). There I encountered warm, nurturing teachers. At Everett Junior High, I was placed in a college prep track. Tracking, as educators know, is a form of intellectual segregation. Out of 2,000 kids, mostly black, maybe 50 kids get a decent education. It's not fair, but I got straight A's—my ticket to Lowell. That's where I realized what a difference a teacher makes.

Her name was Florence Lewis. "Flossie" to her students. After a day in a boring regular English class, I took myself out and demanded to be put in an honors class. I wanted to experience the best, and be put with the best. Flossie obliged.

She didn't just teach, she performed. She communicated. Macbeth? Hamlet? Beowulf? We lived it all in class. Relevance? Not a problem. Sure, maybe she could have taught Carlos Bulosan, the great Filipino American author. But I wanted a taste of the timeless classics. And Flossie made it all real. She made literature a part of my life. I saw the daggers of Lady Macbeth. I grimaced over Hamlet's indecision. Race? Flossie had me convinced that Hamlet was Filipino. MacBeth? He was too. Beowulf was at least part Filipino. In fact, I was sent to detention for slaying Grendel.

Flossie, who at age 74, recently celebrated the completion of her Ph.D. in English literature from UC Berkeley, taught me that literature was a great ladder to new worlds. It wasn't a white world, a black world, an Asian or Hispanic world. Literature liberated the imagination. Flossie took us out of the real world, the literal world, beyond race, beyond the petty politics of school boards and interest groups. It was an adventure into an exciting special place, a universal, intellectual world. Great teachers know how to take you there. But it's hard to get there with bound feet.

March 19, 1998

Clinton, Race, and Spree

As the national conversation on race began last week in Akron, President Clinton indicated that he wanted to mine some real gold. In an effort to move beyond the banal, he wanted candid, honest talk that would make us all feel uncomfortable. "If we don't speak frankly about what we believe, then when it's over we won't feel very good," Clinton said on the national cable broadcast.

Well, the first one's over and frankly, I don't feel very good. Everyone seemed a bit too unwilling to leave their comfort zones.

The president certainly looked comfortable doing his "Dr. Sally Jessy Opra-hue" imitation, proving that he just may be the first president to syndicate when he leaves office. (Can you hear the tease: "Republicans breeding with Democrats on the next 'Bill!'") To his credit, the president did get some people talking and, contrary to what various ideologues believe, talking is good.

In lieu of talking, feelings fester in dark, moist spaces. A type of poisonous fungi emerges. Talking acts as a kind of fungicide. It doesn't make things worse, it airs out the foul odor. So there was a young black man talking about how, compared to a poor white person, he too can put on a nice suit of clothes. He just can't change the color of his skin. There was a white male talking about being afraid of blacks he sees walking toward him. The president thought this was a courageous act, using C-SPAN as a public race confessional. But people did not respond with an, "Amen, brother." The candor only brought on silence.

There were some other frank comments from two Puerto Rican women who complained they constantly get compared to the actress Rosie Perez, the co-star of *White Men Can't Jump*. But few others jumped up to share examples of everyday transgressions involving race. In fact, rather than admissions, the program seemed bogged down by reticence, perhaps even self-censorship. For example, where were the Asian Americans in this dialogue?

Asian Americans were invisible for most of the program. The president was aware of this fact only toward the end. As it became apparent the discussion had turned into a black/white/brown conversation, he was forced to comment, "Before we run out of time, is there an Asian American who wants to be heard?"

What? Yoo-hoo, Mr. President!! What's an Asian American got to do to be part of this national race gabfest? Yell out "Soooooeeeyyyyyyyy"?

Angela Oh, the lone Asian American on the president's advisory panel, told me by phone later in the week that she "winced" the moment she heard the president try to get Asians to speak up. Oh has been unfairly vilified by some commentators for wanting to move beyond the black/white paradigm. To her, the president's comment indicated that unlike other individuals who had been semi-scripted and prepared, Asians seemed to have been an afterthought, marginalized again.

It was several minutes before any Asian American actually did speak up. One of them I deduced to be a graduate of my alma mater, Lowell High in San Francisco. (Could there be any other public high school that is more than 60 percent Asian?) He scored when he talked of being a fifth generation American of Asian descent who was constantly seen as "foreign." At last, an Asian American got in his two cents! Next time, the president needs to get more Asian American voices in to tell what makes Americans edgy about race.

If the president wanted to go out on the edge, all he had to do was mention the Latrell Sprewell and P.J. Carlesimo story.

If the president wanted frank talk that moved us out of our comfort zones, here was the opportunity. Mention race and Sprewell, and nobody—not the media, the Warriors, the NBA, the fans—wants to talk. Not even Rev. Jesse Jackson. It's too hot.

In fact, there was Sprewell, with Johnny Cochran in tow, at a press conference this week saying race was not an issue. He apologized for striking his coach. End of story?

Not so fast. Everyone wants to believe this is merely a matter of a worker crossing the line of authority. A worker hits his boss or, in this case, a black millionaire athlete hits a badgering white millionaire coach. We judge it unacceptable behavior and move on. De facto, Sprewell is wrong. Violence is wrong. His contract is revoked. He's suspended for a year.

But that response conveniently avoids any real attempt to understand the root causes. And it misses an opportunity to examine race as a factor.

This is not in any way meant to condone Sprewell's assault. We're only trying to understand his actions. What really made Sprewell cross the line? Did he snap from' being the lackluster star of a pathetic losing team? Did he believe the extreme admonitions of his coach were a sign of disrespect to a black man who was a recognized star in the meritorious NBA? Where did the anger spring from inside Sprewell? What caused the rage?

People dismiss race in this case because it's not clear cut. Carlesimo used his brash, abrasive style with black and white players alike. But that alone shouldn't absolve him. At the very least, he should be made to examine how he communicates with NBA athletes, 80 percent of whom are black.

As for Sprewell, he lashed out at his white coach and, in the past, black teammates. He threatened one with a two-by-four. So what is he? A universal badass—an equal opportunity offender?

Race did come up in at least one well-publicized Sprewell run-in. In September 1995, as reported in the local press, Sprewell was charged with driving with a suspended license and exhibition of speed two days after he allegedly threatened and made a racist comment to the arresting officer.

The officer was Scott Fukuda, a Japanese American. At the time, Sprewell simply paid the fine for driving with a suspended license. There was not enough evidence to hold Sprewell on the threat to the officer. Perhaps Sprewell's current outbursts could have been avoided if the NBA or his handlers went to the root causes back then.

Instead, the punishment is financial in nature, and summed up as a matter of "accountability for bad behavior."

Bring up race, and you're charged with being a racist. But there's a big difference between exploring race and exploiting it. Johnny Cochran and the Rev. Jackson like to use race like a wild card in a poker match. It swings issues in their direction. But race doesn't help Sprewell.

It only makes him look worse. So they're backing off. Thirty-two million dollars is at stake after all.

Besides, just talking about race here is considered too dangerous, too irresponsible, too divisive. Too uncomfortable. Much easier to participate in a race cover-up. Spree and Carlesimo, just two millionaires disagreeing badly.

It's the kind of thing that undermines the real potential of the president's race dialogue. To get to solutions, Clinton needs the American people to be uncomfortably honest. But that may not be possible at this time in America.

December 11, 1997

All Mixed Up

DEMOGRAPHERS TELL US that minorities will become the majority in America by 2050. Some take it as a warning. Others as a reason to celebrate—finally, a marker on the road to equality.

Actually, we don't have to wait for 2050. In some parts of the U.S., in California especially, there is a new America where ethnic communities are large, but whites still dominate. In California, whites are already less than 50 percent of the state, but still are 76 percent of the electorate. People of color make up over half the state, but account for just a quarter of the voters. Who's leading whom? Why does the New America sound a bit like a new South Africa?

It doesn't have to. Hybrid vigor is in vogue. Inter-marriage—democratic lovemaking—may be the salvation of the New America.

I'm a race mixer from way back. Whites, Hispanics, blacks. I dated them all. But I never dated an Asian. It wasn't a matter of self-hate. It was just a matter of finding someone with whom I wanted to go out. I never went out of my way looking for an Asian. Nor did I exclude Asian women.

My conclusion is that you find love when and where you find it. I found it elsewhere.

Of course, the beauty in any mixed relationship is in the kids. It's the hybrid hope: When we all have a blood interest in each other, maybe we can end the hate.

What's in a Name?

You are what you say you are

O kay, tell the truth. The last time you were faced with filling out one of those "race" identity forms, weren't you tempted to check off something just for fun? Sure, you might be an Asian Pacific Islander, but weren't you tempted to check off African American just for the hell of it? Besides, doesn't Lincoln Lee sound like it would pass for a good African American name? Of course, the truly mischievous would mark "Other Hispanic," while the simply mundane might put an "x" on "white." And why not? It just might get you into one of those Asian-restricted places like UC Berkeley or Lowell High.

The point is, for the most part, race stats are optional. It's based on an honor system. Go ahead, check off anything. They'll usually take your word for it. Which means that even though what you are genetically still counts for something, in terms of official statistics, it's even more important what you call yourself. In these race conscious times, you are what you say you are.

The Federal Government knows it needs a better grasp on the measurement of race and ethnicity, so the Office of Management and Budget has gone over these things systematically with hearings, reports, and its very own bureaucratic organ, the Interagency Committee for the Review of the Racial and Ethnic Standards, a committee so bureaucratic it defies an acronym.

One of the projects for this committee was to figure out whether the terms American Indian or Alaskan Native, Asian or Pacific Islander, black, white, or Hispanic were outdated.

In other words, what DO we all really call each other?

Last May, a survey was conducted of close to 60,000

households "representative of the civilian non-institutional population of the U.S." This means no one asked Charles Manson for his opinion.

What they ended up with are the parameters of politically correct terminology in society. Worried about what to call your pigmented and non-pigmented friends? Why risk offending anyone? With this study you can have the odds on your side.

Here are some of the results: Among blacks, 44.15 percent said they call themselves "black." It was a clear winner compared to the 28.07 percent who prefer the geographically correct phrase, "African American." Only 12.12 percent stuck by the '60s term "Afro-American." Surprisingly, 3.28 percent said they call themselves "Negro," while 1.09 percent still referred to themselves as "colored," and 2.19 percent said they like "some other term." Another 9.11 percent said call me anything, just call me.

Among Hispanics, 57.88 percent preferred to be called Hispanic. Only 11.74 percent preferred the term "Latino." Slightly more, 12.34 percent said they liked the phrase "Of Spanish Origin"; 7.85 percent said they liked "some other term," probably none of which was "El Gordo." Another 10.18 percent said they had "no preference," call them anything, just keep the TV on Telemundo.

Among whites, 61.66 percent said they called themselves "white." Only 16.53 percent said they were Caucasian. A low 2.35 percent cared to be called European American. Less than .96 percent called themselves "Anglos," while 1.97 percent said call me "some other term." Klansman? A whopping 16.53 percent said they didn't care, they were white and whatever they say goes anyway.

Being an Asian American of Filipino descent, I was curious what the study said Asians preferred. But guess what? Not only did they not get Charles Manson's opinion, they didn't bother to get any Asian sentiment on the matter.

What? No Asians? How could that be? Was it because of our relatively small numbers? No. There are far fewer American Indians, and their preferences were tallied. Nearly 50 percent said they preferred that term to Native American by almost 12 percentage points.

So what about the Asians? Was it another oversight? Another slap to one of the most easily ignored minority groups around? Partly.

"We were told it wasn't as great an issue as it was with other groups," Clyde Tucker, the program director of the study, told me by phone from Washington. "Based on our information, what Asians or Pacific Islanders called themselves wasn't particularly controversial."

Tucker acknowledged there were native Hawaiians and Pacific Islanders who are at odds with the "Asian or Pacific Islander" category. But he said that was too small a group to get a meaningful finding in his sampling of 60,000 households.

Of course, he totally ignored other group name issues with the Asian community. For instance, there's the term "Asian American." Then there's "Asian Pacific American." Then there's that artifact that lingers like the term "Negro"—"Oriental." There's the general term, just plain "Asian." And just who gets to fall under that umbrella? Only immigrants and foreign-born? There are even some who would say Arabs and Middle Easterners are "Asian," which certainly makes a case for people who prefer their own ethnic identities. Laotian. Vietnamese. Chinese. Thai. Korean. Filipino. Who is this guy Tucker kidding when he says what we call ourselves isn't "controversial."

Of course it's controversial. And it's a good thing the

census folks are planning more follow-up in the coming year. Because I might just have an identity crisis without an official sense of who we are or what I am.

In the meantime, since no one asked me for my preference, I think I'm going to have to declare my own.

While I like to say "Asian American of Filipino descent," this does not quite describe how 500 years of Spanish Imperialism has dominated my heritage. Nor does it explain how Guillermo is such an Asian name. There really is only one solution. My own group. Filipinos aren't really Eurasians, even though the Spanish are European. The Spanish are really just Spanish—Hispanic. But after considering all the permutations of Hispanic Asian, from Hispasian to Hispo-Asian, I've decided that the Asianness of my heritage must come first. And so I've settled on my own term for me.

As the Godfather of Soul, James Brown, would say, "Say it loud, I'm *As-Panic* and proud." To my fellow As-Panics, next time you see one of those forms, forget "Other." We got a name now.

November 17, 1995

All Mixed Up

The debate on multiracial status gets ugly

Besides inquiring about the number of flush toilets per household in America, there is one major question the Census Bureau gets around to every 10 years. To ethnic communities in America, it is the only question that really matters: "What are you?"

The way you answer that can put an obscure minority on a budget pie chart. Just ask the Filipinos in California. If there are enough of you, members of your group can be catapulted out of "Other," and gain status as a full-fledged bureaucratic "quota." The census is our measure for fairness. If you want your fair share, the census needs to know what you are.

And yet, it's become increasingly difficult to get a straight answer. The simplicity of the question belies its importance. At this stage, here are the correct possible answers: white, black, American Indian and Alaska native, Asian and Pacific Islander, Hispanic, or Spanish. Check the right box. If you fit.

That's the problem. More and more people, especially those with some Asian blood, don't. One box doesn't do it. "Other" isn't enough. We're getting too big for our boxes.

Some activists say the solution is another box labeled "multiracial." On July 20, activists who'd like to see the Census Bureau add such a category are marching to Washington. They want to "publicly and proudly affirm their multiraciality."

That might happen. But what they've already done is expose the new semantics of race politics in America. New battle lines are being drawn. Forget about racist white people, it's the wisdom of Pogo all over again—"I have seen the enemy, and it is us."

Take, for instance, me.

Ask me what I am, and I have a ready answer: "I'm American of Filipino descent." But that's not what I usually say. I certainly don't say I'm "Filipino." Why should I? I was made in America. And I never really say I'm "Asian." In an American context, it still means Chinese. Besides, Filipinos are the most multiracial of all the Asian Pacific Americans to begin with. There's Malay, Indian, Spanish, mixed with a touch of Chinese, even some Japanese. No wonder Filipinos are all screwed up. Instead, I honor the land of my parent's ethnicity, the Philippines, and its location in the world,

Asia. And then I own up to the nasty ravages of imperialism. It is to the Spanish that I owe my last name and my understanding of crucifixion, flagellation, and genuflection, though not necessarily in that order. What else could I call myself but an As-Panic!

It sounds like a whole lot more accurate form of shorthand than "Other." Or anything else I might put down.

But that's me. It's my kids who are in real trouble.

Like many Americans of Asian descent, I've outmarried. The figures are pretty amazing. We outmarry more than blacks, more than whites. We are double-digit outmarriers. Twelve percent of Asian men outmarry. But, that's a small number when you look at Asian women. Twenty-five percent of them outmarry. That's a separate column. Let's just concentrate on the offspring for now. If I'm As-Panic and my wife is Midwest Scotch-Irish-American, what does that make my kids? ASPAMIDSCIRISHAMs? That's one hell of an acronym.

I first noticed the problem when my wife enrolled my daughter in a public school in Maryland. Of course, there was no box for ASPAMIDSCIRISHAMs in the "Official School Form." And there was no box for "Other." When my wife asked a clerk what to put down, the clerk gave the answer she always did.

"Mark the box of the darkest race," she said.

Perhaps that's because of the so-called one-drop rule that has been used to classify blacks. The clerk probably had never dealt with an Asian mixed marriage before. Still, her only concern was that the school get the proper "race credit." My wife's concern was accuracy—the truth.

Silly her, to be concerned with the truth. Suddenly, we are in the world of politics, where the truth is, well, fluid.

This is the dilemma facing every ethnic person in America when confronted with the question "What are you?" Does one answer politically or accurately?

Answer politically, and you accept the big umbrella term, Asian Pacific Islander. It may be unwieldy, but at least we show up on the pie chart. It's totally pragmatic. Just not 100 percent accurate, like everything else political.

So you answer accurately. That may lift your self-esteem, and that of your mixed-race kids. But, oh, the wrath you will incur from the organized civil rights community.

Look at the heartache this accuracy vs. politics dilemma is causing. As we approach the July 20 rally, who do you suppose are the loudest critics of the Multiracial Solidarity March? Well, maybe any hooded KKK stalwart. But, would you figure the NAACP? Would you figure the National Urban League, the National Council of La Raza, and the Lawyers Committee for Civil Rights Under the Law?

I find this particularly troubling. The civil rights community is ganging up on multirace advocates. Gary L. Flowers of the Lawyers Committee is quoted in the *New York Times*: "This multiracial hocus pocus pleases only a relatively few individuals, and for everyone else, it's dangerous. It contributes to the pigmentocracy that already exists in America, that says it's better to be light-skinned than dark-skinned. Will it be better to be multiracial than to be black?"

Pigmentocracy? And you thought my "As-panic" was bad.

The civil rights community is desperately fighting for its life. If everybody did their own "truthful" thing and started calling themselves As-panics or multiracial, the numbers of the traditional "official" Census Bureau groups would be reduced. The NAACP would be out scrounging for members like desperate Amway reps.

Some estimate that if "multirace" were adopted today, it would affect five million people. That's almost as big as APAs at 6.9 million (1990 census). We should feel as threatened as blacks and Hispanics. Except that most of those affected by a "multirace" category would be our kids.

Still, it shows that the civil rights community clearly has not prepared itself for a new day when the issue of race becomes obsolete. That day certainly isn't here, but "multirace" is a step toward the ideal. One world, one race. We're all in loincloths. Living and loving in harmony. Making babies.

Sound great? Sure. So, why hang on to the old vision or, to use the current business phrase, "the old paradigm." That's like the Amish clinging to their buggies, and nostalgic writers to their typewriters. In fact, I'm amazed to hear some bash the multirace trend as ethnic minorities feeling so full of shame and self-hatred that they're hiding their ethnicity, outmarrying in a desire to be white.

Nothing could be further from the truth. Outmarrying is beyond race. It's about love.

But it sure makes the civil rights community uncomfortable. To them, the world is black, white, and racist. Multirace would put the civil rights community as we know it out of business. It's come to need hate and racism more than the racists. Without it, the NAACP becomes the Rotary Club.

That's the sad irony of the new semantics of race politics: Love breeds hate. And race mixing is seen as a bad thing. It's like civil rights leaders have taken a cue from the race purists like Farrakhan. Or Hitler.

July 12, 1996

Diversity's Champ

Tiger Woods and the bold new world

Just look at him. There's something about Tiger Woods that's plain to see: He's a tanned Asian! If he keeps his hat on, he looks kind of—Filipino! Normally there's a tendency to see a bit of ourselves in the hero of the day. But in this case he really is. He's half Asian American. Why can't other people see the Asian in Tiger? Why is he consistently seen as the "black" golfer?

Maybe it's because some people refuse to stop looking in yesterday's mirror and choose to ignore the changing reflection of our society.

With Tiger's emergence, the unbearable truth for some is that he's not just changing the way we look at golf. He's changing the way we understand the issue of race. Not only is he breaking golf records—he's breaking old race paradigms. Through him, we're all beginning to understand that the world isn't just black and white anymore.

That fact alone gave the media fits over the weekend. After he won, reporters and editors seemed incapable of capturing the essential part of Tiger. Great golfer, sure. But what is he? What do you call him?

The first Associated Press story I saw on Woods' Masters triumph contained the basic faux pas. Its lead sentence read: "A black man in a green jacket."

Wrong.

Monday morning, a Bay Area daily contained a similar error when it bellowed: "Tigermania has reached a new level. Young, gifted, a black man in a white man's game, Tiger Woods seemed too good to be true."

The flowing prose was too good to be true as well. You can almost hear an editor say, "Why let the facts get in the way of a good story?" Indeed, a black man dominating a white man's game is a sexy story. Too hard to resist. But it's also wrong.

Calling Tiger Woods a "black man" is only half right. Tiger Woods, by virtue of his Thai mother, Kultida, is also an Asian American. And Asian Americans around the country were as captivated by Tiger's performance as anyone else. Every Asian American I know claims him as kin, even though it seems that every non-Asian deems that connection irrelevant. It isn't.

Arriving at an Asian American friend's house on Sunday, I was astonished to see his entire family sitting in front of the big screen TV, young and old, watching golf. These are people who normally think a seven iron has something to do with the laundry business. But there they were, seeing a little bit of themselves in Tiger.

Some news stories eventually got around to pointing out Tiger's "other side." Some even hedged brilliantly, calling him a black man in the lead paragraph, then mentioning somewhere toward the bottom—perhaps before a mention of second place finisher Tom Kite—that Tiger is, incidentally, an "Asian American."

Credit CBS broadcaster Jim Nantz, who during the CBS post-game interview, caught himself in mid-sentence, when he asked Woods how it felt to be the first "African American" Masters champion. The broadcaster quickly added, "Asian American," to his question.

In fairness to editors, mentioning both Asian American and African American in the same paragraph may have seemed inelegant. But a few papers managed to get the lead right, honoring not just half a Tiger but a whole one. The *New York Times* was one of those papers when it called Woods "a young man of color."

Is this phrasing another example of being, horror of horrors, "politically correct?"

Nope. It's only a matter of accuracy.

In fact, "multiracial" would have worked. But most news editors resist terms like that. To them the world hasn't changed since Jackie Robinson.

They should look at the population statistics. Demographers predict that ethnic minorities will become the nation's majority in 40-50 years. But California is already moving rapidly in that direction. Of the state's 32 million people, projections already show Asian Americans account for nearly four million people, outnumbering blacks significantly. In California, blacks total just 2.5 million. Hispanic Americans are the number one ethnic minority group at over nine million. All told, the state's ethnic minorities make up over 45 percent of the population.

The numbers speak to the undeniable power of diversity. It's a fact. The nation is changing color before our eyes. Yet, how many times do people still see race in this country as a black and white issue?

Complicating the matter further is the issue of "mixed-race" people. The Census Bureau is considering a new "mixed-race" category for the census in the year 2000. Since 1970, births to mixed-race couples have more than tripled, to about 124,000 in 1992. In 1997, it's virtually impossible to merely check off a box on some government form. Race has moved from multiple choice. It practically requires an essay.

Which brings us to the beauty of Tiger Woods. Black, Asian, mixed-race? Watching the media trying to deal with Woods's heritage is to witness the process of racial parameters being redefined. We haven't figured it out yet. We're all still trying. By winning the Masters and forcing reporters to examine their descriptive words, Woods has forced us all to see not just the future of golf, but the future of race in America.

There's something karmic about the Woods story occurring on the anniversary of Jackie Robinson's breakthrough presence in baseball. It's barrier breaking, for sure. But it's just different enough. Robinson fit the simplicity and innocence of the '50s. Then it was just a matter of inclusion. With Tiger, the issues go beyond mere inclusion. They involve acceptance, respect, and, certainly in Tiger's case, acknowledgment of our excellence. He's the perfect symbol for the racial complexities of the next millennium. It's the era of Tiger Woods. The old golf game won't work. And neither will the old labels. As the first person of color to win the Masters, he's diversity's champ.

April 18, 1997

7

Seriously Flip

FILIPINOS ARE BELIEVED TO BE the first Asian settlers in the continental U.S. with the earliest arrival in the 1500s during the Spanish galleon trade. Filipinos jumped ship in Louisiana and began settlements. That was the first. But the real beginning of mass immigration took place in the '20s, followed by a boom after World War II in the '50s and the relaxation of immigration laws in the '60s. The '60s also saw people flee the Philippines during the rise of the Marcos dictatorship. The waves of immigration have contributed to making Filipinos the number one Asian American group in California, and the number one foreign-born Asian group in the country.

"So what?" you ask. That's what happens when you're the Rodney Dangerfield of ethnic minorities.

There are serious issues revolving around respect and identity for the Filipino community in America. Some say it all began when the U.S. duped the Filipinos and stripped them of their declared independence on June 12, 1898. That instilled a colonial mentality that, one hundred years later, many Filipinos still have a hard time shaking.

Colonial Mentality

Whose Independence Day is it anyway?

The biggest challenge to Filipinos of all generations, sizes, and shapes is ridding ourselves of the affliction commonly known as "colonial mentality," or simply "CM."

This is not something you pick up in Boston in a nice pewter. CM is a master/servant frame of mind that puts Filipinos last and makes everything non-Filipino good. And both Filipinos and Filipino Americans can be saddled with it.

Example: among film stars, CM says Meg Ryan, good. Rosanna Roces, bad. (This may not be the best example since the badder Rosanna gets, the more I like it.)

Okay, better example: CM says Ronald Reagan, good. Joseph Estarada, a.k.a. Erap, bad. (Erap at least never co-starred with any monkeys).

But the big one: CM says July 4, good. June 12, bad.

This last example concerns the debate over the real Philippine Independence Day.

Some love July 4 because it's just like America's day. They wrap the flag around themselves as if they were a brass flagpole. They have CM so bad they are in bad need of a case of Viagra.

Some CM Filipinos will say that the U.S. liberated the Philippines from Imperial Japan and (Oh those poor Americans!) lost over 30,000 men to restore Philippine freedom. But they are in denial of the truth.

The only ones who really celebrates July 4 are Americans. It's a fig leaf, a face saver for a failed imperial image of America as world conqueror. Americans gave Filipinos independence on the fourth as a diversion. It's the ultimate in CM. How can you top the triumph of the

British Empire? By making the Fourth of July the Philippines' big day, the failed imperialization of the U.S. in the Philippines becomes just a footnote. That's why Filipinos who honor the fourth do so with spent fire-crackers and half-eaten apple pie.

As a Filipino American, I can't lose. Unless I think of myself as William Howard Taft.

Then I better lose 300 pounds and shave off that stupid mustache.

That's why I honor June 12 as the more honorable Filipino date. You CM folks will try to forget it, but let me refresh your memory.

In 1896, Filipinos battled Spain for the right to genuflect—whenever we damn well pleased. Two years into that fight, the U.S. became involved in a three-month skirmish known as the Spanish American war of 1898.

This was the battle for the Spanish Empire: Cuba, Puerto Rico, Guam, and that necklace of islands in Asia, the Philippines!

Over in Manila Harbor, Admiral Dewey's fleet was at the helm. Filipinos actually helped the U.S. Navy drive the last remaining Spanish troops from the island. Comfortably in control, the Filipinos felt that destiny was their own.

On June 12, 1898, Philippine General Emilio Aguinaldo, essentially the George Washington of his country, proclaimed independence from the balcony of his home in Kawit, Cavite.

Then came the snafu. Though the Spanish American War officially ended with the Treaty of Paris of 1898, Spain was a poor loser. It refused to recognize the Filipinos, and dealt exclusively with the U.S.

The outcome? Cuba received independence. But the other countries were ceded to the U.S. in a deal that cost our taxpayers $20 million. In other words, for a lot less than a baseball team pays for a starting pitcher.

All hail Imperial America! And CM Filipinos bowed.

Aguinaldo's proclamation was totally ignored. On February 4, 1899, the U.S. Army shot at a group of Filipinos to begin a long, protracted American war that historians cite as our first Vietnam.

As the journal, "Anti-imperialism in the United States," edited by Jim Zwick, Syracuse University, points out, the war against the Filipinos was marked by racism and military atrocities.

Aggression and domination were justified through the media. Political cartoons showed Filipinos as savages with feathers in their hair or as grass-skirted Sambos. The Filipinos were obviously wild people in need of colonial taming. By God, we needed a "white father" figure.

In the halls of Congress, Senator Albert Beveridge claimed the colonization of the Philippines as "the mission of our race, trustee under God, of the civilization of the world."

The rhetoric was enough to whitewash the racist bloodletting. A U.S. soldier in 1899 wrote: "Our fighting blood was up and we all wanted to kill 'niggers.' This shooting human beings is a 'hot game,' and beats rabbit hunting all to pieces."

The death toll from America's Filipino foray was staggering: 16,000 to 20,000 Filipino soldiers were killed during the official war, which lasted until 1902. Adding all the civilians who died from famine, disease, and causes related to war, the numbers top off at around 600,000 dead.

On the American side of the ledger, 5,000 GIs died. The remaining members of the American force of 200,000 returned home as heroes and the first protectors of Imperial America.

That's why true Filipinos celebrate June 12. It's the

centennial year. One hundred years should be long enough to fully acknowledge where America went wrong. And if that doesn't make you lose your CM, nothing will.

June 13, 1997

Seriously Flip

A closer look at California's largest Asian majority

It happened again. The *Los Angeles Times* did another one of those mainstream media stories on California's largest Asian minority—Filipinos. It's a story we see over and over again. At least it didn't refer to them as "Sleeping Giants."

Written by K. Connie Kang, a Korean American journalist, I knew the piece would be earnest and sensitive. It was. But I didn't really have to read it.

As a Filipino American, I live the story. I know it so well, I could be Johnny Carson doing a Carnac routine. I could close my eyes, raise the paper to my head, and practically recite it to you verbatim: Filipinos, the largest Asian American group in California, are well-assimilated but lack unity and political power. Blah, blah, blah.

My psychic news sense was right on target. The *Times* headline read, "Filipinos Happy With Life in the U.S. but Lack a United Voice."

But just to make the story look newsy, the *Times* dressed it up with what it described as an "unprecedented public opinion poll of Filipinos in Southern California …" Unprecedented no doubt, because no one's ever bothered to ask them before. In fact, it's probably one of the few times Filipino opinion has really mattered in the

Times. But only because the poll was about Filipinos.

Generally, I distrust polls. How legitimate could the thing be when no one asked me? Besides, polls are to reporters what waves are to surfers. Miss one and there'll be another in a few minutes. Catch one and you have something to stand on. For a second.

Here are some of the questions the *L.A. Times* asked:

Statement: "Filipinos have integrated themselves so much into mainstream American culture that they've lost their own Filipino identity." Agree—43 percent, Disagree—53 percent.

Talk about a loaded statement. Put me squarely in the "Disagree" camp. One can see how the poll uses the term Filipino as a huge umbrella. It doesn't distinguish between "fresh off the boat" immigrants (the FOBs) and the American-reared Filipinos (ARFs). While Filipinos have integrated into society, they will never be truly American. Their cultural ties, like their accents, are just too strong. They can do anything they want. Even become citizens. But sooner or later the Filipino who immigrates and naturalizes here runs into the kind of alienation that tends to make Filipino identity even stronger. My experience has shown that FOBs have trouble forgetting they're Filipino. ARFs have trouble remembering they're Filipino. But they too, develop their own sense of Filipino-ness.

Statement: "Rivalries within the Filipino Community make it difficult for the community to have one strong voice." Agree—72 percent, Disagree—20 percent, Don't know—8 percent.

Petty jealousies are based most notably in one's personality. But they can also hinge on things like which province you're from or what car you drive. Sheer envy makes Filipinos badmouth a rival. Filipinos often refer to it as the "crab mentality." Next time you see some crabs in a pot, see how the one going for the top gets pulled down by the others.

Question: "What do you consider yourself?"

Filipino: 55 percent

Pilipino: 40 percent

Asian: 1 percent

Pacific Islander: 2 percent

Don't know: 2 percent

Since there is no F sound in Tagalog, prideful folks with accents say "Pilipino." Prideful folks who are heard saying "Puck!" are not watching a hockey match. Interestingly, 95 percent prefer "-ilipino." Only 1 percent go with "Asian." No one said "Flip." Regular readers know I prefer my own designation, Asian/Hispanic, or As-Panic.

Question: "What are the most distinctive characteristics of the Filipino people?"

The six most frequent answers:

Hard workers: 37 percent

Strong family ties: 14 percent

Generous: 13 percent

Educated: 10 percent

Loyal: 10 percent

Friendly/Good Natured/Fun: 10 percent

Does "fun" mean "sexy"? If so, 10 percent begs a recount. And what happened to "Short but handsome?" "Smooth-skinned?" Or the natural, "Likes garlic?"

Recount!

Still, as polls go this one's not bad. After all, Filipinos are the whole pie chart. But if the *Times* or anyone else wants to understand Filipinos in America, here are a few tips.

Stop looking for Manilatowns based on a Chinatown or Little Tokyo idea. Town-building just isn't a Filipino thing. Can we all sing "Yes, we have no pagodas?"

Filipinos build families first. In the Philippines, the first towns were formed when families in a particular province banded together. Each family group chose a leader. There was no electoral college. In America, Filipinos have formed de facto Manilatowns, like Daly City in the San Francisco Bay Area. These communities are mainly residential in nature, rather than commercial. Definitely not touristy. No one ever sends postcards from Daly City.

The Filipino community is almost 70 percent recent immigrant. Immigrants determine the public character of the community. I'd include in this group people who've been here 20-30 years. They may be naturalized citizens, but their mentality is still Filipino. The FOBs overrun the second-generation, American-reared Filipinos, those aforementioned ARF types. This schism in the community is the untold story. In fact, the two groups may as well be strangers.

Only the ARFs' nostalgia for their parents' hardship as Filipinos in America really draws them into the culture. Jose Rizal is meaningless. But Dad picking lettuce is everything. The ARFs, after all, are descendants of the earliest Filipinos in America—those of the '20s and '30s who went through anti-miscegenation and discrimination.

The FOBs know little of this history. It's similar to blacks in 1995 who are too young to remember Dr. King. FOBs don't care about history, they're living their "Stateside" fantasy. Miss Liberty is a rock star, and the FOB is her groupie.

And boy do they love to shop. They are consumers par excellence. They still think in pesos, not dollars. So they consume lavishly. They buy all their stateside fantasies. Big TV. Big car. Big rice cooker. Life is good.

As for the group's lack of political involvement? What

for? America is about consumption. In a sense, Filipinos are victims of their own comfort. They have crawled happily to the middle, where they are happy not to rock the boat. They've got what they need: a better life than in the Philippines. What's left to fight for? A voice? For what? To call the Spiegel catalog? Hey, bahala na. C-Span's on mute. What will be will be. They are happy with their lives, and with seeing the same story in the mainstream press. Again, and again, and again.

February 2, 1996

Days of Infamy

Claiming a suspected serial-killer as one of our own

Andrew Cunanan, the suspected serial killer on the lam, may be "public enemy No. 1," but to Filipino Americans everywhere, he's a veritable hero!

Thanks to him, we've all turned white! Right before our eyes. We're not brown, not yellow. We're not a minority. We're white. Cunanan's given Filipinos a "race promotion." The guy's practically our Abe Lincoln. Someone tell the pork council we're the new "white" meat! Filipinos have been "Cunanan-ized."

And that's a major problem. If you haven't realized it by now, Andrew Cunanan's features, his name, his background, and his parentage make him as Filipino American as they come.

His nose is broad and slightly pugged. His name, when not tortured by a newscaster, is not an Irish name, not a form of "cohoon" from the land of lace and limericks. No, it's koo-nah-nahn, a typical surname, a Malayan derivative from Pampanga, a name like Porganan, Alamang,

Pangoringan—all names that are as indigenous as it gets in the islands. The Philippine Islands.

Cunanan was born to a Filipino immigrant who became a citizen the old-fashioned way. His father joined the Navy. The Cunanan family then joined San Diego's huge Filipino American community in the suburb of Rancho Bernardo—known to many as "Rancho Filipino."

While Cunanan's mother, Mary Anne, is Caucasian, from all accounts the family was Filipino. The mixed parentage only makes him a true hybrid, a Filipino American. In fact, Mrs. Cunanan recently returned to another Filipino enclave just outside San Diego, National City. Her charge that Andrew was a gay prostitute elicited this response from his father, Modesto, in the Philippines: "He was not a high-priced prostitute. He had a Catholic upbringing. He was an altar boy!" Ah, a genuflector! Typical Filipino defense. The clues were all there. But the FBI seems clueless.

There he is on the FBI's 10 Most Wanted List: "Andrew Phillip Cunanan. Height: 5'10". Weight: 160-180 pounds. Hair: Dark Brown. Eyes: Brown. Race: White."

Race: White?

OK, sure, 5'10" may be more Filipino than most of us encounter. But that shouldn't confuse anyone on the issue of race. What about Asian American? Pacific Islander? Those terms work for the Census Bureau. Suddenly, Filipinos are white? What am I going to tell my Equal Employment Opportunity officer? The FBI just made my people all honkies?

Filipinos, blessed with a sixth sense of knowing instinctively when a Filipino is near, are going crazy. They are e-mailing and calling me complaining that their media radar screens have been blipping away out of control. Conclusion: A Filipino is present.

Yet, nearly all media accounts and wanted posters with Cunanan's mug describe him as a white person.

While I'm somewhat pleased at being given "white-person" status without having to undergo the strange treatments a la Michael Jackson, I must confess to a little discomfort.

Sure, I'm tired of carrying around all that "little brown brother" baggage—a holdover from World War II, not Louis Vuitton.

But when the news broke, I couldn't help letting out a bit of Filipino pride. "Hey, Cunanan, the alleged killer—he's Filipino," I proclaimed proudly to my white friends. "We're No. 1!"

"No, Emil," they said.

"Yes!" I insisted "Finally, a truly notorious Filipino American! More infamous than Marcos! More famous than Nia Peeples! We've been looking for a politician, or an artist, or a philanthropic businessman. But we've finally made our mark on American culture with our very own alleged serial killer!"

"No, he's white. He's one of us," my friends said.

"That's not fair," I tell them. "Not all serial killers can be white. You can't have them all. Sure, you can dominate other fields. But serial killers, too? Give the Filipino side in him credit for something. Isn't John Wayne Gacy enough for the white race? And you have Dahmer. Can't we have our Cunanan?"

But no, we have no Cunanan. And neither does the FBI. The FBI says he's white. And the FBI's always right. No wonder they haven't caught the guy.

Now they say Cunanan could be wearing a dress. Perhaps not a Versace, more like a Hit or Miss special. The protean nature of Cunanan makes him such a modern-day genius. He doesn't cross just one line. He crosses several. He boggles society's race and ethnicity sensibilities, then he makes crumb cake of our sex and gender notions as well. He's the kind of guy that makes the FBI long for a good old-fashioned Mafia don.

If the FBI really wants to find Cunanan, first thing they should do is start calling him a Filipino American. I think most Filipinos realize their Cunanan-ized "whiteness" is only temporary. They'll get over it. Then the FBI should take the suggestion of their own "profilers" and start looking at communities where Cunanan can blend in and "disappear." Sure, he can hang out in the gay community. But the gay media was on this case a long time before the Versace killing.

Put yourself in Cunanan's high-heeled pumps. If people think you're wearing a dress and hanging out at a gay bar, is that where you're likely to go? The guy's Filipino, not stupid. Take the pumps off.

In the meantime, Cunanan's race mystique points out a few things about modern society. First of all, throw the model-minority myth out the window. Hey, we're badder than badass. Second, if I called Tiger Woods "diversity's champ," then let me call Cunanan "diversity's alleged serial killer." Like Woods, race is a complicated matter. The media, and more importantly law enforcement, don't know how to describe him accurately to the public.

Calling him "white" only shows how truly invisible Filipinos and Asian Americans are in society. Filipino? It's ethnic death. Pure anonymity. No one knows who we are. Or that we exist. We're white by default. When you're on the lam, what could be better than being an Asian American of Filipino descent?

July 25, 1997

Andrew and the Vets

A tale of two Filipino Americans

This week we note the amok-ness of two daring Asian Americans of Filipino descent, Andrew Cunanan and Angel De la Cruz. Both made an impact on the news last week with mixed results. I have sympathy for both.

Cunanan, the suspected cross-dressing serial killer, one of the finest multiple-threat, all-media headliners ever, committed suicide. When a swat team is knocking on your doorstep, life has an odd way of losing its attractiveness.

De la Cruz is one of the Filipino American World War II vets who chained themselves to the White House fence. Mind you, not for fun as Cunanan may have done, but in protest over veterans benefits unfairly denied. There are some in government who wish they would just die and go away.

De la Cruz and Cunanan are players in two seemingly different stories, yet oddly linked historically when one considers the plight of Filipinos in America.

First Cunanan: Some in the community will distance themselves from him, calling him "the anti-Filipino!" A little white blood might do that to you. But Cunanan, the man whom the FBI refused to acknowledge as Filipino, or Asian American, or even Pacific Islander, has a very typical Filipino background.

Born in San Diego to Modesto Cunanan, the family story is typical Filipino American, Navy-style. Cunanan came to this country as thousands of others, in a massive enlistment that provided a way out to many Filipinos. It was the classic immigrant quid pro quo. They lived in Cavite, or Pampanga. Any place with a base in the Philippines. The come on was intoxicating. "Uncle Sam wants you" took on a whole new meaning in the land of mangos and Marcos. Here was the pitch: Join the military, and become a citizen. You might be swabbing decks the rest of your life. If you're lucky, you might get shot at. But consider the benefits. You get to be a second-class American. With the potential of more. That's what real democracy is about. For Modesto Cunanan the military was magic. He became a navy man. And an American. Cunanan married a Caucasian. From that perfect union, Andrew was born.

The military connection was the start of many Filipino American fairytale lives. After the Navy, many Filipinos went on to be proud and productive American citizens. But the Cunanan story, as we know, took on a strange twist. Modesto allegedly became a crooked stockbroker, then went underground in the Philippines. Young, gay Andrew—desirous of fame and attracted to fortune not his own—became the alleged serial killer.

During the tense days after the Versace murder, you couldn't break a nail without Andrew Cunanan's name being mentioned in a universal cry of blame.

"He did it!"

Okay. But where is he? I had said the FBI would never find a Filipino if they insisted on putting "white" on the wanted posters. Accuracy counts for something in these descriptions.

So when the Miami swat team surrounded the infamous houseboat in Miami last week, I thought nothing of it. Cunanan fever was at a high pitch. People were blaming Cunanan for everything from bad traffic to bad breath. When first reports said the police had found nobody in the houseboat, I was in stitches. There is nothing quite so amusing as a multi-hour police stand-off with an empty house. Hey, why stand around when you can sit at a donut shop?

But then the tear gas cleared, and there was

Cunanan. At first, FBI agents couldn't verify his identity by sight. He looked the way law enforcement wants to see any alleged perpetrator. The body's head was blown off by an apparently self-inflicted .40-caliber gunshot. No suicide note was found. Only hours later, did the FBI confirm the body was Cunanan.

The FBI lucked out. To them, the story's over. We won't get any more answers. The FBI's version of the truth is all there is. Serial killings? A white man did it. And a Filipino American is dead.

Story over.

If only the government could be so lucky with the Filipino vets. But Angel De la Cruz, and some 26,000 veterans, many in their 70s and 80s, refuse to die and go away.

Since June, they've staged a hunger strike in Los Angeles' MacArthur Park. When De la Cruz and others chained themselves to the White House fence the other day, it was just another attempt to call attention to the ethical dilemma the U.S. government refuses to acknowledge.

On July 26, 1941, President Roosevelt signed an order that conscripted Filipino soldiers to fight side-by-side with U.S. troops in the Far East. For Filipinos of that era, it was a ticket to paradise. Thousands either volunteered or were drafted into the Army. The magic lure was full GI benefits, just as it was for Cunanan's dad in later years.

The valor of the Filipinos has never been in question. But the integrity of the U.S has. In 1946, Congress passed the Rescission Act, and the promise of America was taken back.

With one congressional act of betrayal, the magic of the military vanished for 200,000 Filipino veterans.

Since 1946, many of the vets stayed on in the

Philippines waiting for justice. Many have come to America to live. Most have died. But 70,000 live on, with nearly half that number in America's Filipino communities. Many of them live in poverty.

Unlike Cunanan, the vets don't get much press these days. Their chains aren't the sexy ones that jump to the front page. Their valient acts, brave fighting in the name of America for a free world, all but forgotten. What did Cunanan do? Assassinate a fashion designer? Was that in the name of freeing us from fashion slavery?

But now there's a growing concern for the veteran's plight. A bipartisan effort is reviving legislation to provide equity to Filipino American vets. Rep. Bob Filner of San Diego is pushing a bill to restore the benefits. But the tab for the survivors could run to $1 billion. A billion sounds like a lot. But in Washington, that's pocket change. Buy cheaper toilets. Cancel some farm subsidies. Just pay the vets their due.

But, despite some positive signs in Congress, there are doubts if the renewed effort will work. The veterans have been ignored because Filipinos in America don't count. And that's where the vets and Cunanan share a bottom line. It's the same old story. When the FBI called the most notorious murder suspect in recent times "White," it only reinforced the sad notion in America. "Little Brown Brother?" Filipinos remain invisible in America.

August 1, 1997

Living History

A voice from the lost generation

Did you forget? October is Filipino American History Month. Fil-a-what?

The Filipino American National Historical Society declared it the month some time ago. Why October? That the World Series is on at the same time is a mere coincidence. This is not a protest over the traditional shortage of Filipino Americans as players or mascots in major league baseball. It would be fair to say, however, that October does mark the first time a Filipino "crossed home plate." The first Filipino, a refugee from the Spanish Galleon trades, is known to have set foot on American soil on October 18, 1587, in Morro Bay, near Santa Barbara, California. His first words, I imagine, would have been something like, "God, I'm wet." In tagalog. This "first Filipino home run," as it were, makes the AWOL sailor part Jackie Robinson, part Neil Armstrong. One small step for Filipinos. One giant step for immigrants. Certainly a cause to celebrate. But as you may have noticed, the celebration in October has caught on about as well as Filipino American History Month.

That's too bad because Filipino American history is about all of us. Notice the "American" portion of that phrase. We're not talking about how the Filipino chief, Lapu Lapu, killed the Spanish imperializer Magellan, or any of that stuff. That's Philippine History. We're talking about American history, which depicts what happened to Filipinos once they came to America. Not surprisingly, it's like any immigrant's tale, a work in progress filled with hardship and discrimination. To understand the history, you don't even have to read a book. You just have to talk to a Filipino American. It shouldn't be that hard. There are almost two million of us in America. We all have stories, and we're all a part of a history little known to non-Filipinos.

For example, there's Fred Basconcillo of Daly City. Fred is one of those "missing Filipino-Americans," a member of a lost generation. He's 58, talks without an

111

accent, and is American as apple pie. He's also as Filipino as lumpia. He even pronounces his name the Filipino way: "Bas-con-SEEL-Yo," and not the Spanish way: "Bas-con-see-YO." He's a rarity. You just don't find many Filipinos born in America who are in their 50s. Here's why: Most Filipinos immigrated to America in the '20s, when Filipinos were patronized as "Little Brown Brothers" and exploited as "Little Brown Workers." My dad, Willie, immigrated in 1927. Fred's dad, Artemio, immigrated in 1924. Most of the men were students—pensionados. Or they were recruited as farm laborers to work in California camps. My dad posed as a student, but ended up in restaurant work, in the pantry were it was "cooler." Fred's dad came over with some farm labor-ers who were initially shipped to Hawaii. When they ended up in San Francisco, the workers usually found themselves 10 to a South of Market apartment, in essen-tially all-male communities. The ratio was as high as 16 men to every one Filipino woman. Considering that inter-racial dating and marriage were essentially out-lawed, the situation made for some pretty lonely nights. About 30 years worth for some.

It wasn't until after the war in the 1950s that entrance quotas were lifted on Filipino women. Suddenly, these 50-year-old Filipino bachelors were making hay, marrying, and starting a Filipino baby boom. That explains my birth.

But Fred, and more specifically Fred's dad, got lucky. Artemio Basconcillo married after a relatively short peri-od of time. Fred was born in 1937, almost 20 years earli-er than me. Fred's dad beat some high sociological odds. Little wonder he would go on to run the hottest gambling joint in the 10-block strip on the edge of Chinatown

"That was my dad's place, the New Luneta Cafe," Fred beamed as we drove by Kearny Street last week. "That place was jumping. There was Tino's Barber Shop, and the International Hotel. Next door to the cafe was the Bataan luncheonette. And across the street was the Golden Gate. It was all Manilatown. "

In toney establishments around the city, Filipinos weren't even allowed in. But Manilatown was theirs. And the gambling attracted high rollers of all races. People like then Mayor Jim Rolph, the city attorney, and the city's biggest politicos, all Caucasian. "I got pictures of them all," Fred said.

It was a hot time. Fred was doing okay himself. He remembers working as the kitchen help at the brothel of San Francisco's famous madame, Sally Stanford. It was his dad's connections that got him the job.

One day young Fred asked his dad: "If we're doing so well, why aren't we rich?"

The older Basconcillo sat his son down and explained to him that most of his money went to helping and supporting Filipino contract workers who had escaped the farm labor camps in places like Watsonville and Salinas.

"It was like an underground railroad," Fred said. "These guys would come live with us for a few weeks, and then disappear. They were all my 'uncles.' I got a new one every few weeks. My dad was bankrolling them, so they'd have an equal chance and wouldn't be deported. It was like he was betting on their lives. I had no idea at the time this was happening." All Fred knew is that despite the good times on Kearny Street, being Filipino in America was no easy thing. Filipinos were sometimes welcome, most times welcome mat.

For those of Philippine descent, October is to the time to recall the price and the pain of being Filipino in America.

October 27, 1995

Mother for the Ages

Oh, baby!

Come on. Level with me. When you first heard about that 63-year-old woman who gave birth—believed to be the oldest living thing ever to lay and hatch an egg—didn't you wonder about the woman Saddam Hussein would have surely dubbed "The mother of all mothers?"

What's the background of this world-record holder? Is she rich? Is she a welfare mom? Is she costing us anything? She got an egg loan—did she get better terms than Newt Gingrich? And of course, there's the most important question in these race-conscious times: What box did she check off on all those bureaucratic forms after the delivery? What is the ethnicity of this iron woman? In what language did she yell out the magic word in the delivery room known to mothers of all races and ages: "Epidural!"

A 63-year-old woman enduring the pain of birth? This mother's got to be an "Other."

How else could she do it? There are age limits. 55 was the cut-off age at the University of Southern California Program of Assisted Reproduction. Surely, they card you upon entering. The fact that she got in shows the biological urge is nearly as strong as the urge of the underage to drink beer.

But, the doctors said, this woman claimed to be 50 when she began the fertilizing process three years ago. She was really 60. And she passed. There could be only one explanation.

She was a Filipina. As an Asian American of Filipino descent, I have come to observe the aging process of my fellow Asians. The timeline in general goes like this: You spend a lifetime looking like you're 16, until you reach 50. And then you look like you're 50 until you reach 84, at which time you begin to act your age.

Sure enough, my suspicions were confirmed, by no less plausible a source than the British tabloids. The 63-year-old mom is Filipina. An Asian American. There were no pictures, but the woman was described as looking 15 years younger than her age.

I asked an expert about these matters—my Mom, a Filipina immigrant who at 80 would not exactly be described as "spry." But just question the possibility and propriety of a 63-year-old Filipina giving birth, and I swear you'd think I'd insulted the mother country. "Why, I could have had one into my late 50s. I was still having my cycle then," she said to me proudly. "And looking pretty young, too, I might add."

Sheesh. Okay, Mom, you could have been a contender.

But for now we have the newly crowned mother of the ages, Arceli Keh, from Highland, Calif., 60 miles east of Los Angeles, who gave birth last year. Married for 16 years, her husband, Isagani, is 60. And they have no other children. Keh described herself and her husband as "working people" who are "far from wealthy." They spent at least $50,000 dollars for the process, the cost of about two years at Harvard. So Isagani still works at the carpentry shop to pay the bills. And though the British newspaper, the *Express*, reportedly paid no money, the Kehs say the bidding for their story starts at $200,000.

But this isn't about money. They're happy with the natal results. After three attempts, Isagani's sperm fertilized a donated egg from a younger woman. The outcome was young Cynthia, a 6-pound 4-ounce baby by Cesarean section. Read all about it in the current issue of *Fertility and Sterility*. Sexier than it sounds, it's a magazine one really does buy strictly for the articles.

Since the announcement, Keh's delivery has spawned a new era of ethical concern. Is it proper for one to give birth at that age? And let's not be sexist: Is it too selfish on the part of both aging parents?

Having been born to older parents, I'm somewhat conflicted. My immigrant father was 50 when he "sired" me. It was after World War II. You can do the math. At age 10, I was afraid my fastball would hurt him when we played baseball. I started going to A's games by myself at age 11. At age 12, I would go to father/son events alone. Like many children of Asian immigrants, not only was I much younger, my English skills were better—in fourth grade. I ended up being my own parent. Which wasn't altogether such a bad thing. I didn't believe in corporal punishment. But I did miss having a father. I had a grandfather.

It wasn't until I learned that the delayed families of Asian Americans, specifically Filipino, could be traced back to the institutional racism of their day. When anti-intermarriage laws prevailed, and women of common ethnicity were limited in number from immigrating, there were few options for the burgeoning bachelor society of Asian Americans.

Since learning the history, I've softened my earlier assessments of my father. But now I can't tell him that. He died nearly 20 years ago.

I've come to know that racism may have prevented him from achieving his potential. But it didn't deny him his biological potential—to have an American family. Many Asians have heard their parents boast that their "family is their wealth." And perhaps this is the way we should evaluate Arceli Keh.

"I wasn't trying to make history," she told the *Express*. "I just wanted to have a baby."

She could. And she did. So how much of the intense criticism toward the Kehs comes from a race or cultural

116

perspective? The differences between Asians and others in terms of the reverence for the old is well documented. If the old want to have babies, is there a problem?

It seems that most of the white commentators come with the notion that the modern mom is the svelte, active blonde in the mini-van, shuttling kids from school to Brownies to ballet, doing a little aerobics class in her spare time. Who's to say that the modern-day Madonna and child, the "Soccer Mom" with kids in tow, is the only acceptable version of motherhood?

For the Filipino immigrant in particular, childbirth is like the completion of the journey. It's the creation of an American legacy. Ultimately, the birth of young Cynthia is a triumph not merely of science and biology, but of the immigrant's drive to be fulfilled.

May 2, 1997

Filipinos in the Fields

A neglected story of the farm labor movement

A new documentary on the farmworkers movement airs next week on PBS. *The Fight in the Fields: Cesar Chavez and the Farmworkers' Struggle* is a pastiche of news archival footage with present-day interviews that offers an excellent chronology of the farm labor movement.

It's worth viewing, but as is often the case with documentaries, it leaves one begging for more. The documentary begins auspiciously by showing how the farm worker fight was really one of modern society's first multicultural battles, with the so-called "Okies," blacks, Asians, Filipinos, and Mexicans at odds with growers. But the film ends up as a deification of the Chicano hero, Chavez.

Focused on Chavez, the two-hour documentary follows the path of most popular histories of the movement. It would have been nice to see a fuller acknowledgment of Asian Americans in the development of the union. In fact, it was the Filipinos in the fields who led the way.

For example, everyone knows and honors the greatness of Cesar Chavez—disciple of Gandhi, friend of the Kennedys, saint, martyr, and Chicano labor leader. They name streets after guys like him.

But has anyone ever heard of Larry Itliong?

Larry who?

What about Philip Vera Cruz? Big V. Big C.

How about Pete Velasco?

Hardly household names, but names certainly worthy of being mentioned in the same breath as Chavez.

Call them the Big Three—Itliong, Vera Cruz, and Velasco—pioneering immigrants from the Philippines, among the first wave that arrived in the United States in the '20s. They are the so-called manongs, the name given to the Filipino old-timers. They numbered around 50,000, mostly young men barely past their teens, who came seeking education and enrichment. Vera Cruz and Itliong had intended to be lawyers. Instead they found they were brought to fill America's need for cheap labor in fields and factories up and down the West Coast. They first arrived in Seattle and found their way to the canning operations in Alaska and the Northwest.

In the '30s, Itliong helped establish the Alaska Cannery Workers Union. He ran for office under the slogan "militant, frank, and capable." His drive and determination helped the union get a contract that called for an eight-hour day plus overtime. But a migrant organizer's work is never done. Itliong moved on to California.

Vera Cruz worked the canneries too. Then in the '50s he migrated to the fields of California. Together with

Itliong, who had formed the Filipino Farm Labor Union, and Velasaco, the three became the soul of the Agricultural Workers Organizing Committee (AWOC). With more than 30 years of experience organizing workers, they were a stalwart force.

Growers found out quickly. When Coachella Valley growers cut wages during the harvest, AWOC spearheaded a force of striking Filipino laborers that won a major victory for farmworkers there. That was in 1965, B.C. Before Chavez.

As grape season ended in the Coachella, the Big Three, already in their 50s and 60s, migrated further up the state to the vineyards in Delano. On Sept. 7, 1965, more than 1,500 Filipinos of the AWOC voted to strike.

Where was Chavez? He was trying to figure out his next move. He wasn't ready to strike anywhere. But the Filipinos were already striking and winning contracts. And now the talk was of a new strike in Delano, where the majority of the state's table grapes are grown. Chavez took his cue from the Big Three. A week after the Filipinos voted, 5,000 members of Chavez's predominantly Mexican National Farm Workers Association voted to join the Filipinos. A year later, the two unions merged, resulting in the United Farm Workers Organizing Committee.

The film presents a subtle but different shading. It mentions the Filipinos' successful strike in the Coachella Valley. But it also implies that when the talk of a strike moved northward to Delano, the Filipinos were half-hearted, and didn't want to join the picket lines. At best, the film makes the Filipino leadership sound indecisive. It quotes Itliong referring to the Filipino rank and file: "Well, they said we don't want to picket our boss, we've been working for him for 10-15-30 years. We don't want him to be mad at us."

Not exactly.

Chicano Studies Professor Rodolfo Acuna of Cal State Northridge said in the *Los Angeles Times*: "The Filipinos were the ones who pushed [the union] into the strike. They were the more militant ones. They were later eclipsed by the largeness of the Mexican labor force. But you really have to give them credit."

They have received little.

The film uses a clip of Itliong that doesn't capture his fire and determination as an organizer. And Velasco is brought on to speak piously of Chavez. But at least they're in the film. There is no mention at all of Philip Vera Cruz.

Vera Cruz's absence in the documentary is telling. Honored in his lifetime by the Smithsonian Institute and the AFL-CIO, Vera Cruz, a UFW vice president, died in 1994 at the age of 89. Before his death he published a memoir in 1992, *Philip Vera Cruz: A Personal History of Filipino Immigrants and the Farmworkers Movement*. In it he was highly critical of Chavez.

"Cesar didn't give credit to the Filipinos, even in the beginning," Vera Cruz said. "Do you think we did anything? We were the first ones to sit down in the fields. That sure enough is proof."

Vera Cruz was also critical of the UFW's lack of democracy and neglect of the Filipino old-timers, the majority of whom were retired by the 1970s.

But the last straw was Chavez's visit to the Philippines in 1977 during the time of Marcos and martial law. "We in the union believed in the general principles of freedom," Vera Cruz said. "Cesar's trip to a dictatorship was in direct contradiction to those principles we stood for."

Chavez never addressed the issue. Vera Cruz would later resign from his role on the UFW board.

It's great that the filmmakers made such a reverent piece on Chavez. But the story of the Asian Americans in the farm labor movement, the first successful strikers, the Filipinos in the fields, is an oft neglected tale worth greater recognition. Certainly, Velasco, Itliong, and especially Vera Cruz are Filipino heroes worthy of mention in the same breath as Chavez.

April 11, 1997

Diversity on the Diamond
Filipino in the outfield

It's World Series time, and though NBC Sports honchos seem bored with the Indians-Marlins matchup, this series does present some intriguing storylines on America's diversity.

For example, it's a safe bet that Pacific Asian Americans, with their love of seafood, will be rooting for the Marlins, whose team logo is a big fish (with what looks like a toothpick sticking out of its mouth) connected in a Siamese-fashion with a big "F."

This "F" could stand for "Filipino." But it doesn't. Still, it makes for a somewhat "existential" World Series for Filipinos, considering that "F" does not exist as an official letter in the Philippine language.

At least now you know why baseball-loving Filipinos everywhere can be heard screaming, "Go Pish! Go Pish!"

Unfortunately, early on, the Pish look like pailures. When the Indians rocked Miami ace Kevin Brown in Game Two, the Marlins looked like "dried fish." Had they lost that championship "moisture?"

Of course, you could be rooting for the Indians, which brings us to Diversity Storyline No. 2: What about

Cleveland's pesky mascot problem?

I mean, isn't that Indian mascot insulting to Native Americans? In the past, protests have been lodged against more egregious variations: Redskins, Injuns, Braves. Thank goodness, the Braves with their "Tomahawk Chop" didn't get into the series. Not only does the move make the entire stadium look like a Jane Fonda workout tape, but it would have really brought the "politically correct" out of the woodwork. In fact, a Braves/Indians final would have made the series impossible to enjoy for fear of oppressing indigenous peoples. Thank goodness for the Fish.

Still, I've managed to come to terms with the Indian mascot: the over-dentured Chief Yahoo, the guy on the Indians' caps, the smiling caricature with the one feather sticking out of his smiling head. It's a cartoon character, no malice intended. To get worked up over that is like the SPCA getting upset with a Warner Bros. cartoon over the exploitation of animals. Or like white people protesting the portrayal of Elmer Fudd.

In fact, I've noticed few Native American protests, perhaps because this year's series stars a number of people of color. There's Livan Hernandez, the Marlin's Cuban fireballer. Tony Fernandez, the Indian's ALCS hero. There's Alomar. Vizquel. Ramirez. Bonilla. Grissom, Sheffield. Latinos and blacks dominate the series. Abner Doubleday's game is showing a little diversity on the field.

Especially noticeable is how the countries involved in the Spanish American War have produced tremendous baseball players. Cuba. Puerto Rico. The U.S.

There's just one country missing. The Philippines.

Where are the Filipino baseball stars?

We know of Asians in the majors. Hideo Nomo is Japanese, as is the Yankee's Irabu. Chan Ho Park is Korean. All of them major-league pitchers of Asian descent playing baseball. No Filipinos.

Which brings us to perhaps the most interesting angle of all, Diversity Storyline No. 3: The World Series coincides with Filipino American History Month. And what better way to honor the moment than by saluting a unique bit of American sports history—the first pure-blood Filipino American in the Major Leagues.

He's a true pioneer, a real beeg leeger—Bobby Balcena.

Bobby Who? Balcena. For the hard of hearing, that's BAL-SEENA.

He didn't last long enough to get an elaborate nickname other than "Bobby." But if I were writing or anchoring sports, the first Filipino American ball player would deserve at least a handful of nicknames.

Start with Bobby Bolo (killer knife). Bobby Balut (fertilized duck egg). Or the Bermanesque (as in ESPN's Chris Berman) Bobby "Have you ever Bal- CENA Filipino play outfield?" Or the more compact, Bobby "Hit the Ball"-cena.

Something would have stuck. How about simply Bobby Ball?

The period from 1948 to 1962 was the era for Bobby Ball. Imagine, a full year after Jackie Robinson broke the color barrier, the first Filipino through was Balcena. At 5'7" and 160 pounds, he was standard-issue Filipino. *The Sporting News'* pre-computer, typed-out bio reads: "Only full-blooded Filipino in pro ball." He was indeed a rare breed, a member of that lost generation—born in San Pedro, Calif., on Aug. 1, 1928. Because of anti-miscegenation laws and a lack of Filipina women, most full-blood American-borns weren't even conceived until the '50s. But who could deny Bobby Ball!

As a strapping 20-year-old fresh out of the Navy, the World War II vet played 102 games for Mexicali in the Sunset League. He threw left-handed, but batted from the right side. And what a bat. He hit .369, with eight homers, 81 RBIs (Runs Batted In). In 1949, he did even better: 180 hits in 123 games for a .367 average, 16 homers, 132 RBIs. The guy had some pop.

Balcena moved up each year. Originally the property of the St. Louis Browns, he played in Wichita (.290, 82 RBIs) and San Antonio (141 games, 145 hits). Then pre-Major League Toronto and Kansas City. And two eye-popping years in the Pacific Coast League with Seattle, hitting above .290! In 1956, at age 28, he had 14 homers, 38 doubles, 62 RBIs, a .295 average. No affirmative action was needed here. He was ready for the bigs.

The Cincinnati Reds, the sluggingest team in the majors with 221 homers and stars like Frank Robinson, Ted Kluszewski, and Wally Post, gave Bobby Ball a nine-game apprenticeship.

On Sept. 16, 1956, late in the season, Balcena debuted. In Cincinnati next to Kluszewski, they probably thought he was the batboy. But the record showed he played seven games, with two official at-bats. He struck out once, and got no hits. He finished with a perfect .000 batting average!

Nevertheless, Balcena was an impact player. Somehow he got on base. The record shows no walks, no bases on balls. He must have pinch run for some lumbering slowpoke because the record reveals Balcena's contribution to Major League baseball: two runs. He scored twice! He touched home!

Balcena did not make the team in '57 and was sent back to Seattle. But the rigors of the pro game took its toll on the Filipino body. Injuries plagued our hero. Bobby Ball was unraveling. He played five more years in Buffalo, Dallas, Vancouver, and Hawaii. He never got called up to the bigs again.

Balcena died in San Pedro on Jan. 5, 1993, at age 64.

But Bobby Ball lives on! As the first Filipino American pro baseballer, he was a historic first. He's in my Hall of Fame, my Mr. October.

October 23, 1997

Sisters

I DIDN'T MARRY AN ASIAN WOMAN. It was merely a case of who was accessible. In many of my personal and professional situations I was the only Filipino, the only Asian in the vicinity. I just never met the right Asian woman at the right time.

But you must commend me. At least I didn't go out and buy one.

Today, Asian women continue to be bought and sold as commodities. They are indentured servants, garment workers, contract workers. And then there are the domestic versions—a combination of cheap labor, cheap sex, and wife as "man's best friend."

The buyers are all lured by an exotic image that says Asian women are compliant and subservient. The outcome is a double whammy of racism and sexism.

Buying Thai, Selling Low

Slave-trade immigration

Whenever Asians make national headline news it's worth noting. And this week's stars are the nearly 70 Thai women in southern California who made it to the front page of the *New York Times* last Friday.

They weren't the slim, high-heeled Thai beauty queens you often see. Nor were they scholars, nor Asians with high grades and test scores who couldn't get into their first-choice University of California campus. These women would have gladly chosen UC Riverside.

Most definitely these women weren't the Asians used to justify the abolition of affirmative action at UC. In fact, when Newt Gingrich and Pete Wilson were grieving for the poor Asians who were hurt by such a heinous social program as affirmative action, they probably weren't even thinking of these headline Asians.

They should have been. Because these are the victimized Asians who can really use some help.

The nearly 70 Thai women were garment factory workers rounded up in El Monte, Calif. Immigration and Naturalization Service officials who conducted the raid described them as victims of "involuntary servitude." That's an eight-syllable phrase that means the Thai women were slaves.

On the front page of the *Times*, the squatting women looked like deer caught in the headlights. Oddly, they are more representative of the plight of Asian Americans in this country than we all think.

The women lived in a two-story house that looked fairly normal for El Monte. Some of them lived there for years. There were bars on the windows. But heck, everyone has a right to enhanced security. The dead giveaway should have been the razor wire above the fence, the kind I've only seen at places like New York's notorious city jail, Riker's Island. That's when it should have occurred to someone that more than for keeping people out, the bars and razor wire were for keeping people in.

According to officials, the workers were brought over to the United States by some Thai entrepreneurs. If people didn't have money for the trip, they could work it off. Funny how that doesn't get done so easily, even if you're forced to work long hours at half the minimum wage. Call it the bamboo handcuffs.

Each night when the women finished, they would be locked up and guarded. If they tried to escape, they would be threatened with physical harm or death. According to one grand jury affidavit, two people were said to be severely beaten and sent back to Thailand. Another was routinely abused. Threats of reprisal against families in Thailand were commonplace. Lucas Guttentag of the American Civil Liberties Union's National Immigrant Rights Project called the situation "as bad as any incident that I have heard of, especially in terms of the amount of time the immigrants were locked up."

The crime is a serious one, with eight people charged in a federal indictment. By their names you can learn another sad fact about these crimes: Sunee Manasulangkoon, Tavee Uvawas, Sunton Rawungchasiung, Rampa Suthaprasit, Suporn Verayutnilai, Seree Granjapiree, Hong Wangdee, and Thomas Panthong. Asians are both predator and prey. Talk about dog eat dog.

This is something we've seen in our other groups. With more and more Filipino seniors coming to America with newly granted veterans status, a number of Filipino "entrepreneurs" have opened up "veterans homes." In exchange for the new arrival's Supplemental Security

Income check, the veterans homes are run like little prisons. At least the veterans weren't asked to sew.

That wasn't the case with the Thai women whose garments were sold by some of the biggest names in the retail industry. Officials found labels from such retailers as Macy's, Hecht's, and Filene's. There is no way to tell if the retailers knew of the sweat shop labor. But in this case, ignorance served as a kind of bliss. No retailer has been charged as an accessory.

It's hard to imagine a defense for this kind of exploitation. But let's try. In the world of Newt and the Republicans, can the Thai fellows running this racket be blamed for prospecting their "warm market" and coming up with such a moneymaking scheme? Would any self-respecting white businessperson do any differently if he or she spoke Thai? What were these guys doing, after all, but offering a service in the capitalist tradition? With so many clothes in our top stores being sewn in Asian countries, does it make a difference if the Asians are doing the sewing in such decrepit conditions in America vs. their old homeland? These Thai guys were just paraphrasing an age-old business adage: Buy Thai, sell low.

In a legal world where even O.J. gets a defense, I'm sure the eight indicted won't have any problem finding someone to argue their position.

And what of the Thai women? They were released. But to what? Will they get any better treatment from the legitimate world? Will they be deported? Or will another set of Asians stalk them as prey?

Seeing them on the front page of the *Times* made me feel that they could have been the poster children for the entire disenfranchised Asian American community. We should all forget the model-minority image. Despite our bona-fide success stories, Asian America remains an America of immigrants who remain vulnerable, exploitable. They remain the base of our exploding numbers. We shouldn't let our success blind us to that fact.

August 11, 1995

Grooms Wanted

A business proposition for '90s mail-order grooms

They're killed in Seattle; beaten in Minnesota; romanced, married, and impregnated by Oklahoma City bombing suspects. Mail-order brides seem to attract the world's best customers.

While it would definitely be in my amok nature to speak out against the exploitation of Filipino women, consider how trite that would be. I mean, these are the Gingrich years. Exploitation itself should be a free market.

So let us not condemn it. Let us use it. Keep in mind that the catalog-shopping industry is booming with people buying everything from the Fruit of the Month to the Panty of the Month. Mere consumables. But hey, a mail-order bride is forever! Or rather it should be, with a little "product satisfaction." It's a competitive world out there, and there should be some "product control." Why doesn't anyone advocate some consumer protection besides condoms?

If you are a Filipino considering entering the mail-order-bride business as a career, relationship, or citizenship move, perhaps you should first consider that life in the Philippines is not all that bad compared to some things. However, if you seek adventure, remember that, be it mail order, retail—heck, even wholesale—the customer is your friend.

But beware, these are fragile guys. Guys who consider triple-X 900-number conversations mature relationships. Guys who have just graduated from inflatable dolls.

And then there's the politics. They think Hillary Clinton would be better with a little less air. They think the U.S. government is being taken over by foreign agents who will take away their guns. They're like fish served American style—without the head. Here's a tip for you: when your new husband asks you to decorate the living room in camouflage, you should know that this does not mean "French provincial."

When these men licked that stamp to summon you, they were really trying for normalcy. They were reaching out, trading in a few parcels of freeze-dried chili for whatever tuyo (dried fish) you could bring to the table. And they got you. You came in the mail.

But treating these sickos with a little fried rice and kindness isn't going to help them, nor is it going to save the Filipino stronghold on the mail-order-bride business. For the mail-order-spouse industry to expand and grow, it must develop new market niches.

With that in mind, I think we're ready for something big. The next hot thing, bigger than multilevel marketing, bigger than fast-food franchise opportunities like "Bagoong King." My friends, are you ready for mail-order grooms?

Why should Filipino women be the sole object of exploitation? Don't Filipino men deserve to see their share of the underside of America?

By the same token, why should white American males be the only ones to show off their seedy unsociable side? There must be some kinky white women desperately seeking a "smooth-skinned native boy" willing to be a spouse-*cum*-love slave at the drop of a green card.

Dare I ask whatever happened to equality? This mail-order-bride business has been a sexist one-way street for way too long.

Why can't white women—heck, women, period—participate in this mail-order fun?

Just think: if American women wrote to Filipino guys, maybe we'd get some good love letters going in the penpal stage. American women wouldn't have to copy Elizabeth Barrett Browning's love poems like all those horny white guys who race to the library to transcribe some corn. (They're the ones who think that Tom Clancy writes sexy romance novels.) I'm sure the women attracted to this deal would bring to it a rhetorical savvy all their own—just the thing to lure the adventurous Filipino guy, the mail-order groom.

What a deal both ways! Look what a few love letters would get you: Docile, smiling guys who like to cook. Guys who, pound for pound, are maestros of the mattress, or the back seat, or the banig, or the kitchen table—wherever love strikes. The Filipino mail-order groom aims to please.

Somewhere in the Philippines he's out there, looking for love in all the wrong places (although the cockfights aren't exactly what I'd call a high-odds places to find unrequited love—unless you're into blood and feathers). And somewhere in America there is some corn-fed, socially underutilized white American female who is tired of playing with her glow-in-the-dark, battery-operated Ken doll at night. She's had it with the Neanderthal American male; she is ready to be served. She's ready for a Filipino guy!

Who'd be interested in short brown guys, you ask? Someone who knows that a mail-order groom is short everywhere but in the love department. Besides, what is height good for anyway? Reaching for the Spam at the top of the cupboard? Why do you think God made ladders?

I know. Now you're asking, "How do I sign up? How

133

can I be a groom?" Or you're wondering, "How can I be groomed?" Well you've come to the right place, because as the instigator of this exciting new love conduit I can offer sample descriptions of several mail-order grooms for potential suitors who are bona fide Americans.

Mail-order groom No. 1: "Bong-Bong" loves to wear barong tagalog pants. No gold teeth. Likes poetry, basketball, and cable TV. Grows vegetables in spare time. Has more spare time than vegetables. Pays no taxes!

Mail-order groom No. 2: "Imeldo" loves shoulder pads, politics, and pansit. Does karaoke to country-and-western music. Thinks country refers to Laoag. Drives jeepney at night. Hobbies: carves Virgin Mary figurines from Ivory soap bars.

And this is but a partial list. Send your pictures now. We will end the sexism in the mail-order spouse business! Exploitation, after all, should be an equal-opportunity affair.

September 1, 1995

Barbie's Make-Over

She's not your average China doll

The day after Thanksgiving marks the beginning of the gift-buying season, when consumerism dominates the spirit and people start thinking of shopping as an Olympic sport.

If you're a parent, this means you'll be shopping mostly for toys.

I know these things. I'm a father of three small children, two of them little girls. Tamagotchis? Old news. Beany Babies? Come on, get with the program. Hello Kitty? Hello ancient history. A good parent is already looking forward to next Christmas. That means one must keep abreast of all the toy news that comes out. What's Saddam and his blinking? It just doesn't rate with the earth-shattering news this week about a certain t-o-y. And boy, was it a shocker.

Barbie's getting fat and going flat. On purpose.

Mattel announced the plastic beauty is undergoing a major evolutionary overhaul. Her waist will be wider. Her chest will be normalized. So as not to throw her proportions totally out of whack, her hips will be thin, a kind of "pre-septuplet, non-childbearing" thin.

Though her measurements will shrink, there will be no corresponding rise in her IQ. She won't be any smarter. But she'll still be wiser than the people who see 8-inch plastic figures as realistic models for human beings. To them, the new Barbie standard is to make the Barbie shape more "attainable."

As a smart consumer, I am on to this marketing strategy. Who doesn't realize that "Breast Reduction Barbie" is just an excuse to follow up with a spin-off: "Implant Barbie." Now your Barbie can have the operation all the gals in Hollywood are getting!

Likewise, "Wide Waist Barbie" is just an excuse to bring out "Liposuction Barbie," the doll that actually lets you suck out her fat with your very own straw! Kids really need something more challenging than the standard dolls that actually replicate infant wetting cycles! How can Barbie compete with "Baby Eat and Wet My Pants Again." By the time girls are older, shouldn't they progress to "That Time of Month Barbie?"

Probably not. But "Suck Me Skinny Barbie," the liposuction Barbie, has a certain ring to it.

An ingenious bit of marketing, indeed. Making Barbie perfect was apparently too limiting. After all, what modern woman is perfect? Modern woman is into striving. Now Barbie can be every bit as neurotic as the modern woman. Barbie is the imperfect doll yearning for perfection.

Frankly, though I've heard that feminists are cheering "Fat Barbie" as some revolutionary breakthrough, I don't buy it.

If they really wanted breakthroughs, there are a few things Mattel could have done besides making it look like Barbie eats Big Macs morning, noon, and night.

For starters, they could have given Barbie a brain. Why not update the talking doll concept. You know, the "pull my string, and let me wow you" doll. Nobody's really fooled by it, but then again, there are some people who think these dolls are actually role models for humans.

Why not put a digital chip in Barbie that lets her speak her mind. Imagine a Barbie that says something provocative like:

"I don't eat red meat. Have you ever heard of e coli?" Ah, the Veggie Barbie.

Or how about the "Ethnic Studies Barbie," a Barbie that, among other things, acknowledges history and current trends, like the one toward multiracial coupling: "I'm white but my boyfriend's an Asian American rap singer. He's sort of 'Cablanasian,' like Tiger Woods. Oh, by the way did you know there's no such thing as a model minority. And being part model, I should know."

And to keep that new waistline nice and thick, Mattel definitely should have the "Taco Bell Talk-to-the-Drive-Through-Attendant Barbie." Pull its string and it says: "My boyfriend's a gangbanger." Or: "I'll have some hot sauce, Vato, with my big burrito, and extra sour cream please."

For the more traditionally inclined, the new thick-waisted Barbie could also come in a more sedentary, graduate student, book-wormy version, one that could say: "I really doubt that Shakespeare was Sir Francis Bacon. By the way, do you have any bacon? I'm famished."

Mattel wouldn't have the stomach for that kind of realism. By comparison, making her fat and flatter is nonthreatening. Like turning Barbie into a young Martha Stewart.

Finally, there is one more thing I would have done. I would have made Mattel acknowledge Barbie's roots.

I'm not talking about her fake hair color. Or making Barbie ethnic. What's that after all, but a superficial matter of mixing the right paint.

No, I'm talking about something more deep-rooted-and serious-than all her commercialized blonde facades like the "Pet Doctor Barbie," "Dentist Barbie," "Hollywood Barbie," et al. I'm not into her "scenario." I'm into her heritage.

Go ahead and rip off her clothes. Then look, you'll find it inscribed in her plastic bod plain as day. Just like the majority of toys out there, Barbie's *Made in China*.

You might find an Indonesian one in the bunch. Doesn't matter. Barbie, the plastic all- American girl is some kind of Asian. And more often than not Chinese.

It seems to me that if people want realism, it's a shame to be hung up with the size of Barbie's breasts. Why not talk about the laborers who gave birth to Barbie in China and how badly exploited they were?

As a Chinese girl, Barbie is one of the few to make it out of China alive these days. With China's one-child-per-family policy, there have been reports of families choosing to kill off infant girls in favor of boys.

In fact, research by University of Washington demographer William Lavely shows how the ratio of boys to girls in China has risen dramatically in the '90s. Lavely's census figures from 1995 show that 9.6 percent of girls are "missing." Of this percentage, 15 percent can be explained due to mortality, and the rest are due to "unknown causes." It shows that people are taking active steps to end the lives of infant Chinese girls. There have been reports of sex-selective abortion, and the drowning of baby girls, but no outcry.

It's ironic that Mattel is worried about damaging the self-image of American girls who play with plastic dolls when the society Mattel pays to make the dolls is murdering its daughters.

We can't kid ourselves and say the girls got out and are really Barbie dolls. But Mattel could do a lot more in the name of realism than worrying about Barbie's breast size. It could focus on a tragedy that's being internationally ignored, and give Barbie a conscience. The world is ready for a "Human Rights Barbie." That's more than a China Doll.

November 27, 1997

Asian Wonder Women

Thank goodness Michelle Yeoh is on the scene in that new James Bond film, *Tomorrow Never Dies*. Extreme feminists might say they should have made her James Bond and ditched the hair-helmeted, spy mannequin, and all his techno-gizmos.

But honestly, isn't giving Yeoh the Bruce Lee part revolutionary enough? Please, one major paradigm shift at a time.

Frankly, to this Asian American male observer, the thought of Yeoh as "Bond Girl," kicking some white male ass in the Battle of the Sexes, is oddly satisfying.

A foot in the groin is just what some of these guys need to break free of their outdated notion of Asian women.

138

Guys like Terry Nichols and the late Larry Hillblom.

Nichols you know as the convicted bomber and managing general partner in the bombing firm Nichols/McVeigh, coming soon to a penitentiary near you.

Hillblom was a reclusive multi-millionaire and founder of the DHL air courier service, who died in a 1995 plane crash in Saipan, probably in search of virgins.

Both Nichols and Hillblom are the latest examples of White Male Swine who share a common vision of Asian womanhood. The problem is these guys got the wrong 'hood. The only way the bespectacled Nichols and Hillblom could have gotten it so wrong was to have smeared Vaseline on their glasses first.

How else could they have envisioned Asia as the last depository, the mother lode if you will, for black-haired beauties who are the perfect examples of servile, virginal, uncorrupted femaleness? What attributes! All that and they have the look of exotic porcelain dolls!

It's become the new chauvinist ideal of feminine virtue—especially among white males. Why be stuck with some sagging, aging "girl next door" who has transformed herself into a whiny, complaining "equality monger" hell bent on redefining the term "community property"?

Dump her now and go Asian, where the women are compliant participants in the traditional male/female equation, the "Me Tarzan, You Jane" idea of gender fairness, where women learn that it's their right to be thankful that men have soiled enough items to make a decent load of laundry.

Less than a full load? Don't despair. Laundry is but a portion of an unrelenting day that includes cooking, child care, and cleaning. But it's all worthwhile come the end of the day when the benefits of the job kick in. That's when the Asian woman greets her imperial man and performs her duty of loving, husband service. All done gratefully with a smile. The Asian female way.

When you actually find this fantasy let me know.

Nichols thought that the fantasy was all attainable with a few postage stamps. Why settle for an inflatable doll when you can get a mail-order bride? In 1990, Nichols was a typical candidate. Fresh from divorce at age 35, he was looking for some loyalty and warmth. Someone or something that didn't require rabies shots and flea powder. He went straight to the Philippines and registered with a mail-order bride agency. In Cebu City, he found the perfect Asian woman—Marife Torres, the virginal 17-year-old daughter of a traffic police officer.

Unfortunately, when his order arrived a year later, Torres was practically postage due. She was six months pregnant with another man's child. This is called getting the mail-order marriage off on the wrong foot.

But there is no money-back guarantee in this game. You can't complain to the Federal Trade Commission. The Nichols trudged on. And after seven years of marriage, the true test of love came during Marife Nichols' testimony at her husband's bombing trial.

She was the trial's best witness. But not for the defense.

Marife testified that in 1995 she was back in the Philippines considering ending the marriage and returning to school. She made a condition of her return that Nichols not spend time with McVeigh.

"I got jealous of him ... Terry would spend time with him," she said. It's one thing to be a football widow. But a survivalist/militia widow?

Marife also testified that she traveled to gun shows with her anti-government husband. She sold guns, boxes of those gourmet-packaged military meals, and 8-ounce plastic bottles of ammonium nitrate fertilizer. The kind that could be made to go boom.

140

But most damning of all, she told prosecutors Nichols lied to her and kept her in the dark about hanging out with McVeigh. Bye-bye alibi.

As for the late multi-millionaire Hillblom, he was a man who had become totally obsessed with young teenage virgins from the Philippines, Vietnam, and Saipan. He was quite productive too. Four young women who worked in bars and nightclubs in Asia claimed to have been impregnated by him. Hillblom's untimely death in a 1995 plane crash started the "Have you been with Larry?" fan club. The charter members—the kids of these tycoon/go-go dancer relationships, including two Filipino girls, a Vietnamese boy, and a Palauan teenager—all claimed a share of Hillblom's multi-million dollar estate. And they had DNA tests to prove it.

While the kids lived on just over $100 a month in Asia, Hillblom's estate contested their claims in court. Finally, after nearly two years, the estate settled for a reported sum of $90 million per child. Four others whose mothers claimed relationships with Hillblom will get $1 million each.

Do you think at the very least Hillblom's estate wishes he had used condoms?

These stories of the last few weeks may read like the "Revenge of the Asian Virgins," but it's far from a Male Swine wake-up call. Don't bet on things changing significantly. Impoverished Asian girls are still working in bars, all too willing to sell their bodies to get to a better place, orgasmic or otherwise. Others are still more than willing to go postal, taking their chances that their mail-order prince will be Johnny Depp and not Terry Nichols. But one wonders if they'd all go legit if there wasn't this prevalent strain of fantasy—a White Male/Asian Female thing—lurking out there looking to be fulfilled.

That's where Yeoh-mama, Michelle Bond-Fu, comes in. She can be of service to mail-order fantasists and virgin conquistadors everywhere. Nothing like a well-timed heel to the groin.

January 15, 1998

9

All in the Family

EVERY FAMILY HAS ITS SECRETS—the weird aunts and uncles who once lived in the basement.

The Asian American community is no different. It's just that our weird aunts and uncles are generally a much larger group of people than any of us realize. It's a nationality of people. Or it's a sexual minority. Or newcomers. And more and more, we're asking them all to come upstairs and sit at the table, with the "regular folk."

This chapter is about having a realistic and honest assessment of the community. It's something that's often lost as Asian America ponders its public image.

You see, we all want to think we're perfect. The general public thinks so. That's how myths like "Model Minority" got started. It's the glorification of the "good Asian" stereotypes, the ones that say how rich, healthy, and successful we are.

But it's not nearly so rosy for many of us.

Then there's the immigrant factor from all parts of Asia, with groups that come into American society from another world. They make the Beverly Hillbillies seem genteel.

The list goes on. Cross-dressing gay Asians. Big, hearty Pacific Islanders. Just when you think you have us pegged, the notion of what is Asian Pacific American comes roaring back with a new image of diversity that makes you see the term in a totally different way. It's a rich mix. And that's nothing to be ashamed about.

Immigrant Makeover

The model minority myth gets the full treatment

In the late and not-so-lamented CBS prime-time sit-com, *Pearl*, one of the main characters was an Asian Pacific American female college student. She's typically "model minority." She knows all the answers, never goes anywhere without her laptop, and has the personality of an onion cake. Exotic. And flat. But beautiful.

Considering the vast audience that tunes in to a sit-com each week, you might say the Asian American character is the image that launched a thousand stereotypes. Thousands upon thousands, in fact. And in the minds of many, the show's Asian American will be as close as any of them will get to an Asian this week. Don't know an Asian? The one in *Pearl* is good enough.

But is it a real depiction? It doesn't matter. Add another model-minority image to our American culture Hall of Shame. It's all the dominant culture really wants to know about us. We are smart, test well, and—APA women, at least—come across quite well. Next. Society is impatient. It has its acceptable images for every minority—blacks, Hispanics, Asians. And that's that. Why bother with reality when society is all too willing to accept our PR?

Thank goodness, then, for another study that takes a shot at presenting the Asian American "warts and all."

This one was put together by a consortium of 55 Asian community agencies in the San Francisco area.

Guess what it discovered? Asian Americans are among the poorest residents in San Francisco, often at risk when it comes to health and education matters. Isn't that wonderful? Some model minority.

This study absolutely turns upside down any presumptions generally heard about Asians in the mainstream. For example:

- Are Asian Americans upstanding members of the middle class and above? Maybe some. But don't forget the rest of us. Census data shows that more than a third of the city's families living in poverty are APAs. A third! Yes! 33 percent. This is more than from any other ethnic group. This is such a jarring, alien notion, so different from mainstream thinking about Asians, that one can't help but double-check whether the words are printed properly on the page. They are.

- Are Asian Americans the bookish types, the straight-A kids who love school? Kids who are like that character in *Pearl*? Consider that the study found that one of every five San Francisco youths who drop out of high school is Asian. That's a double-digit dropout rate. Sure, there may be Asians winning all the awards at Lowell High School, but who's bothering to reach out to this considerable number of APA dropouts in San Francisco?

- Are all the Asian kids whizzes at deciphering *Hamlet*? Sure, if they're in advanced-placement English. The reality is far more startling. In San Francisco, APAs make up the largest ethnic group in the San Francisco school district. Nearly 39 percent feel they don't speak English well enough to succeed academically.

We're in transition, folks. And that means the stats are going to be even more eye-popping in terms of health care. As we go from old country to new, our health is going to be a reflection of where we stand in the transition. If you're stuck on the idea of the good APA doctor and the upstanding upper-middle-class family, take a look at what the San Francisco study found about APA health:

- APAs make up the largest group of low-birth-weight babies—28 percent. That's according to San Francisco Department of Public Health Statistics.
- APAs have the highest rate of active tuberculosis.
- APAs are heavy users of San Francisco's mental health programs. In 1993-1994, African Americans made up 38 percent of those who used mental health clinics; Asian Americans constituted 30 percent.

Healthwise, what can be said? We're small. We're sick. We're crazy. Yes, we're going amok. It's obvious isn't it? We're cultural and social misfits. And yet, no one seems to understand why. Remember, we're the model minority.

Programs for our community fail to get the funding they need simply because the perception is stuck on an old image of sane, dull, prosperous Asian Americans. In fact, policy-makers have given short shrift to Asian nonprofits because of a lack of perception about the community.

This new study from San Francisco goes a long way toward helping that perception problem. Studies like it show how the massive, recent immigration of Asian Americans is re-making the image of the community. The stereotypes of old may be based on earlier immigration, topped off by second-, third-, fourth-, even fifth-generation APA achievement. The old stereotype no longer applies.

Immigration and its huge numbers obliterate the stereotype and redefine a new reality. We're poor, sick, crazy. And we don't speak English well. We're struggling. And we're vulnerable. Unfortunately, without studies like this latest one from San Francisco, the mainstream is totally oblivious to our "Immigration Makeover." Society is so slow to pick up on it, it's still trying to figure out the semiotics of *Flower Drum Song*.

The quiet, overachieving Asian American has been replaced by the misplaced, misunderstood, underachieving Asian immigrant, more often a legal immigrant, and a naturalized one. The new stereotype is not of the straight-A student, it's of the foreigner trying desperately to belong. The sooner we all realize that, the sooner we can place the final nail in the coffin of the model minority.

October 4, 1996

That Lump in the Oriental Carpet

Pacific Islanders get swept under the rug

Here's a good bar bet for the long lull between karaoke victims (the songs, not the singers). For the whole tab, name all the Pacific Island groups, not necessarily in alphabetical order. Okay. Let's see. There are Samoans. And Fijians. And . . . did I say Marlon Brando? Didn't he become an island?

Fans of Brando, Gauguin, and Junior Seau, may be able to identify a few of the 22 groups that populate the hundreds of islands speckling the Pacific. But there's always an elusive one that floats away. (Did I say Alcatraz?) This weekend, you can experience them all through food, culture, song, and dance at the Pacific Islander Festival at San Diego's Marina Park North.

"Don't forget the Caroline Islands in Micronesia," says Hanalei Vierra, a Hawaiian shrink and men's group leader ("no drum beating"), who serves as chair of the festival. He's referring to the group of islands east of the Philippines that includes the Yap Islands, where talk radio probably flourishes. Vierra estimates that of the 350,000 Pacific Islanders in the U.S., about 20,000 live in

San Diego. Chamorros from Guam in the Melanesian Islands are the most numerous. Hawaiians, Samoans, and Tongans from Polynesia follow. And then there's Fiji in Micronesia, along with the aforementioned Carolines—so small and forgettable, they could be dubbed "Amnesia."

Last year Vierra, a member of the Ahahui Kiwilla Hawaii O San Diego, or "Hawaiian Civic Club," was given the task of coordinating the San Diego visit of the Hokule'a. It's a replica of the kind of twin-hulled sailing canoe that sailed the open Pacific nearly 2,000 years ago. Europeans had their tall ships. The Chinese had their junks. Pacific Islanders had hokule'as.

"These guys were on a hollow canoe with nothing," says Vierra. "No maps, no compasses. Just cloud formations, knowledge of currents, and bird sightings."

In other words, they were up a proverbial creek without a paddle. In an Asian sense, I guess, it would be like balancing the federal budget with an abacus. In any event, they still got to their destination. Not that they had one really.

("Imagine sailing out there not knowing if you were ever going to hit land," Vierra says in awe. "These Polynesians discovered everything in the Pacific. And this was all centuries before Columbus and Lief Ericson. These Islander guys were good.")

As ocean voyagers, the Polynesians sailed a thousand miles just from Hawaii to Tahiti. And because the canoes linked the islands and their people in a powerful way back then, Vierra recognizes today how the visiting canoe could make for a powerful symbol of community pride. "When I realized what it represented, I saw the Hokule'a as something special to celebrate in a way we've never done before. In public, together."

Which has always been the problem. Pacific Islanders don't exactly have a high profile. Never mind Junior

Seau (NFL Samoan) or Alfred "Superbowl TD" Pupunu (NFL Tongan). For the rest of the group, physical stature is inversely related to their public stature.

Then again, it's not as if they've been routinely encouraged to be anything but low profile. For many years, Pacific Islanders were grouped as "other." Recently, they've been grouped as the aforementioned "P" in APA—a.k.a. Asian Pacific Americans. The all-inclusive term, however, often has the bureaucratic effect of shoving Pacific Islanders under a rug. Vierra and others notice the big lump in the center. This is the lump that others rarely see. But Vierra doesn't want to secede from the APA distinction totally. He just wants you to understand that distinctive lump. It's different.

"Some Pacific Islanders may have links to countries like Japan or the Philippines, but those countries are really more a part of Asia. They are Pacific Rim people, not Island people," Vierra says. "The Island peoples are the indigenous people of the Pacific, with unique cultures all their own. And with unique needs. When we're lumped in [with Pacific Rim peoples], Pacific Islanders get nothing."

For the most part, their lack of recognition in all arenas is stunning. Though Guam and American Samoa have representatives in Congress, they are nonvoting members. Now Vierra hopes the canoe will do for the community what nonvoting members of Congress have not: Build a sense of pride that will empower Pacific Islanders to achieve a more prominent role in society at large.

Politicians have been quick to respond. Heck, even Gov. Pete Wilson, between bashing affirmative color-blindness and running for president, has proclaimed July 17-23 "Pacific Islander Festival Week" in San Diego. Suddenly people notice that lump in the rug.

July 21, 1995

149

Cheesehead Justice

One verdict on the Hmong

If you haven't yet lost faith in our American justice system, particularly in its ability to deal with Asian Pacific Americans and our unique pathologies, just hang on a second.

Did you hear the one about the Hmong child molester?

Regular readers of mine will note I have written about our dear Hmong brothers and sisters before. The Hmong, as you know, are perhaps the Asians whose American experiences most resemble the sitcom, *The Beverly Hillbillies*. They are simple mountain people who've moved so much in their lives that their main defense has been to resist any change in context. As refugees they have been flung into situations in which they are more than mere "aliens." They are out of this world. This, of course, naturally creates situations that are, at times, comic.

For example, a good many Hmong live in Wisconsin. Knowing that Wisconsinites lovingly refer to themselves as "Cheeseheads," I've noted that the re-location of Hmongs to the area have given rise to the "Cheesehead Hmong."

More often, unfortunately, the mixture of the Hmong among the Cheeseheads has only given rise to tragedy, the most current example being what I call a case of "Cheesehead Justice."

Recently, a jury in La Crosse, Wis., found Sia Ye Vang, 32, of Detroit guilty of four counts of first-degree sexual assault involving girls who were 10 and 11 years old. They happened to be his stepdaughters. The girls testified they were assaulted at their home by Vang between 1992 and 1994.

I repeat, the jury found Vang "guilty."

So, what kind of sentence do you suppose Vang received? This should be a no-brainer, especially during a time in which criminals are scum—even lower than immigrants. This is a time when the phrase "three strikes and you're out" applies more to our courts of law than to the baseball diamond. Considering all that, how could anyone expect anything but the harshest sentence for Vang? He faced up to 80 years in prison for being found guilty of first-degree sexual assault. Throw the book at him and a few extra chapters, right?

Wrong. On Aug. 21, Circuit Judge Ramona Gonzalez sentenced Vang to 24 years probation and gave him the right to return to Detroit. No jail time. No striped uniform. No breaking rocks with a sledgehammer. The judge did place conditions on his sentence. Vang is under orders to remain employed, perform 1,000 hours of community service, stay away from the victims and their families, and—here's the grabber—take English lessons.

Sentenced to English lessons? Talk about hard time. I always knew my English teachers were somewhat warden-like, but I never thought I'd see the day when sentence diagramming would be rightfully recognized as punitive.

It was a brilliant save for the defense, which skillfully played its race cards. Attorney Katherine Schnell used the Hmong cultural defense to the hilt. Here's what she told reporters: "In an agrarian culture sometimes young girls are married, and that may have been a carry over in their culture. In our country that happened not too long ago, young women were coupled. This behavior may have seemed to be OK or not as bad as we view it."

Except a jury did find Vang guilty.

So what's the judge's excuse? According to reports, she was staying the sentence "to allow him the opportunity to continue in his education and his assimilation into our culture."

What? So that he could molest again in English? I don't think this is what the English-only folks had in mind.

Mind you, I've been practically pro-molester on all the current, fashionable anti-molester proposals that have been proposed. I'm against registration and picture books of local molesters which deny molesters who've served their time to live in peace and a chance to resume a normal life. And, most definitely, I'm against chemical castration, which does not address the true violent nature of the molester. I am for tougher laws, and not letting them out in the first place until they're ready to be let out.

The Vang case didn't address any of that. Not his psychological state, his need for counseling, or his propensity and desire to molest.

The case only addressed molestation as a cultural problem. Like it was a peculiarly Hmong thing, or Asian thing. The judge's remedy was a sentence based on culture. The judge practically said: "You may have molested in your culture, but not in ours, Mr. Hmongman. Learn English. That way you'll only conjugate verbs. And you won't dangle your participles. Now get out and don't come back until you can recite *Beowulf*."

It all points out the inadequacies of the law and how the scales of justice often don't balance when dealing with our cultural differences. The judge, I'm sure, was trying. But she got it all wrong. Judge Gonzalez actually cited Vang's consistent denial of the charges (What's he going to say?); Vang's good standing in the community (How would she know unless she were Hmong?); and comments that one of the victims didn't want him to go to jail.

English-only folks take note. In this situation, an

interpreter or anything that would have enhanced communication would have helped tremendously. In the end, the judge was hopelessly lost when she said, "There is no doubt in my mind that something happened, and no doubt that they hate him. But I am perplexed that these girls do not want him to go to prison."

Actually, it was a statement from an uncle who vigorously claimed he was misunderstood. "They interpreted my statement wrong," Ter Yang told reporters. "I never said the girls didn't want him in prison. I was saying in my own words that they didn't want to see him going to prison, but that he should be punished for his crime."

Culture may call for leniency in some cases, but not in child molestation. The Hmong may do some crazy things, but child molestation is a crime in any language. So, for now, chalk up a victory for the "Hmong as backward people" defense. It worked. Of course, the system failed the little girls, now 14 and 15. And it failed to address the problems of a molester, now free.

September 6, 1996

Going GAPA

Cross-dressing for pride

Some people get jury duty. This week I get to be a judge. Not like the Ito Man—a different kind of judge.

Yes, Lady Justice will still be my model. And the blindfold will still stand for some legal virtue and not for any sort of kinkiness. But there will be a catch. Lady Justice will be a guy in drag. I've been tapped by the Gay Asian Pacific Alliance (GAPA) to judge its annual beauty pageant.

Initially, I had some problems with such things. But

with some coaxing, I've become a convert. To beauty pageants, that is.

This is a big affair in San Francisco, a city known for its fruits and nuts, just as Hawaii is known for its prickly pineapples and jaw-breaking macademias. Why did they tap me? Believe me, it's not due to experience. Nor is it due to how good I look in a black robe. I openly admit my knowledge of gay beauty is limited. For a while, I was still in denial over Rock Hudson. I will say, however, that I agree with most people that aesthetically Michelangelo's David is preferable to, say, an overly muscled Arnold Schwarzenegger type. Why? David is rock, even when he's not excited. Arnold could get soft. Utility counts for something. Thank goodness that, as a card-carrying heterosexual, I know a little more about women. Which should help me in the lesbian competition.

That's because GAPA is an equal-opportunity pageant, with both Mr. and Miss GAPA divisions. Supposedly the Miss division challenges gender conformity; the Mr. division challenges notions of Asian male masculinity. The pageant is like a nontraditional casting call for the Village People. (Hmm, an Asian as the Indian Chief? Now that's worth pondering.)

Personally, I'd like to see members of the two divisions put on the gloves and headgear and duke it out. It would definitely be more entertaining than the last Tyson fight. But then that would be a boxing tournament and not a beauty pageant.

Secretly I think they have a beauty contest because there are a lot of Filipino guys who run the pageant, like Voltaire Gungab, the fellow who asked me to judge. Why this is so I can only speculate. Perhaps it's because in the Philippines beauty pageants rank right up there as a sport—after basketball, cockfighting, and fighting for the Marcos millions.

This, of course, is quite the opposite stand that many people, regardless of sexual persuasion, have of beauty pageants. The tendency these days is to downgrade these affairs as degrading fetes of sexual objectification. That is why Miss America officials insist they're running a scholarship program. All I know is that I got a scholarship from Harvard and they didn't ask me to parade around in heels and a one-piece.

So you can imagine my initial reluctance to participate. In the pageant, that is. GAPA officials proudly say they've had the pageant for seven years. And it's only gotten bigger. Said GAPA guy Dino Duazo: "It's a way of fostering self-awareness, identity, and camaraderie among its members. We continually set out to expand perceptions that others may have of us. This gives us a way to create our own image, define our community, and present it with pride."

Sounds high-minded, but at first I wasn't sure. I mean, to me the only thing the event seems to foster is stereotypes. I can't think of anything more stereotypical than a gay beauty pageant—except, of course, a Liberace record swap and bake sale. I especially wondered about the need for this campy contest, considering that acceptance of gays in the Asian American community is growing.

In *A. Magazine*'s recent sex poll, 50.4 percent of heterosexuals interviewed found homosexuality totally acceptable. Fewer than 20 percent of heterosexuals said homosexuality was somewhat or completely unacceptable. And then there were the 15.4 percent who claimed no opinion, possibly due to the fact they had their heads in the sand or had yet to meet Mr. or Mrs. Right—or Wrong, as the case may be.

These are encouraging numbers, yet they still don't make up for the discrimination, low self-esteem, and social awkwardness that are still a part of life for many Asian American gays on the mainland. If you add to that list gay-bashing, homophobia, and general harassment, you wouldn't confuse the mainland for paradise, let alone a gay mecca.

There are places that are slightly more progressive. In Hawaii, the state has found the denial of same-sex marriages to be a violation of one's civil rights. The Hawaiian state supreme court even ruled that marriage is a basic civil right. The move toward the recognition of same-sex marriages in Hawaii means that gays might finally be able to live happily ever after.

On the mainland, however, gay Asian Americans fight the tremendous burden of being some combination of an ethnic, a sexual, and a gender minority. That's three strikes for some. And homophobes tend to see double. States are beginning to pass laws that would allow them to ignore any gay victory in Hawaii.

So the GAPA pageant is on. It's fun and campy, but it's also one of those in-your-face kind of events. Subtlety will be penalized. Therefore, I'm taking my role as judge quite seriously. Of course, my eagle eyes will be on the lookout for cross-dressing contestants. No double-dipping allowed.

And I'm putting special thought into every beauty pageant's climax: the questions. You know, those final questions the judges ask that turn contestants into bumbling, tongue-tied fools in heels. The aforementioned Voltaire Gungab, whose name sounds like an organization of French guys philosophizing about semiautomatic weapons, gave me some examples from previous pageants, most of which were fairly tame.

"If we were to go out on a date, where would you take me?" (Depends on whose expense account.)

"If you were a fruit, what would you be and why?" (This

is an opportunity for the contestant to refer to bananas.)

"What are your special qualities that make you a good lover?" (Here's where the candidate can show concern for safe sex, hygiene, and general humanitarianism.)

Out of a sense of conscientiousness, as opposed to sadism, and in the spirit of competition, I was initially determined not to throw any softballs. I'm going to make them hard questions, I thought. I'm a judge, after all.

But then I figured these guys have seen enough hard times. They deserve softballs—the softer the better. So from me, they're all going to get round fat ones. Let's see how far they can hit them out of the park.

It all should make for a hearty good time for the gay Asian American community, the kind that tends to boost a sense of pride. The kind that tends to blast away the pain of being Asian American and gay.

September 8, 1995

10

Our Little ACDC Problem

IT'S BEEN SAID THAT the campaign finance scandal flopped with the American public because there just wasn't any sex in it.

So I put some into it. I made it sexier: ACDC, or The Asian Campaign Donation Controversy.

My initial reaction was to protect the innocent against spurious and xenophobic claims in what was undoubtedly a partisan rush to judgement.

I had no undying loyalty to Huang, Riady, et al. But I was always skeptical of leaks and media speculation. Let the investigative process find the truth, and let the culprits be prosecuted.

What happened is quite different. Asian Americans were treated far more harshly than non-Asian contributors, some even singled out just for having Asian names. Meanwhile, white campaign abusers got a free pass from the media. No one else got "The Asian Treatment." The general coverage, dubbed "China-gate" or "Indo-gate," slurred an entire community.

But now Trie and Chung have plea bargained and are cooperating. Chung has admitted to getting funds--$300,000 from an officer in the Chinese military. An Asian connection? Perhaps, but that doesn't make us all guilty. AC/DC is about a few Asian Americans who went both ways--East and West.

The Middlemen

The newly arrived want to get there fast

We have an AC/DC problem, folks. And it's a real scandal of identity.

Oh, that's AC/DC as in Asian Campaign Donations/Controversy. And it goes right to the core of what we're about, if anything, in American society.

With each passing week, there's another name, another subpoena, and a lot more dollars. Welcome the latest entry, Charles Yah Lin Trie, a Little Rock, Ark., restaurant owner and longtime Clinton friend. Trie used to serve up lunch-time potstickers to then-Gov. Clinton, something that identifies him as a bona-fide, dyed-in-the-wool F.O.B. (Friend of Bill).

Trie solicited and gave nearly $640,000 dollars to President Clinton's legal defense fund. But because of questions as to the money's original source, it was all returned last week. It was also revealed that Trie used his influence to get Wang Jun, head of a Chinese gun manufacturer, an invitation to a small, intimate White House gathering.

Just the prez and a handful of F.O.B.s. Little did he know one of them really was an F.O.B. The standard kind.

As a foreigner, Wang is prohibited from contributing to American campaigns. Oh, and did anyone notice that Wang's company, Poly Technologies, was under federal investigation for smuggling 2,000 Chinese-made AK-47 assault rifles with a street value of $4 million into the U.S.?

President Clinton called it "clearly inappropriate," and had to get out his best spin-face to address the matter. "I have no recollection of meeting him," Clinton told reporters. "I'm not sure he ever said anything."

It is not clear whether the president was commenting on our community's general invisibility, or our docile nature. Or if it was a specific reference to Wang's scintillating personality, his modest skill in English, or his personal hygiene. But we must credit the president for not saying, "Asians? Seen one, seen them all."

For good measure, the president added that he's not guilty of anything. "I can tell you for sure," Clinton said of his non-meeting. "Nothing inappropriate came from it, in terms of any governmental action on my part."

Is that like not inhaling? As for Wang and Trie, they're on their own.

Still, it's another fine mess stemming from our community's AC/DC problem, and it's growing. Last week the Justice Department subpoenaed the White House and the DNC for all records, including visits, correspondence, and telephone calls involving more than 20 individuals.

Besides Trie, the individuals include the initial AC/DC figures: Democratic fundraiser John Huang and the Indonesian moguls James and Mochtar Riady of the Lippo banking conglomerate. Huang raised more than $3 million this year. So far, $1.5 million has been returned as questionable.

But the real tragedy this week may have been UC Berkeley Chancellor Chang-Lin Tien coming up empty handed. Touted as a possibility to become the first Asian American Cabinet member in history, Tien, an engineer by training and an energy scholar, was on the short list for Energy Secretary. But several reports citing sources close to the nomination process claimed that Tien's ties to Riady doomed the nomination.

Did Clinton have a choice? Tien obtained a $200,000 donation from the much maligned Mochtar Riady to help build a university building. Riady also wrote to Tien on behalf of three family members who sought admission to

UC. Two were admitted; one was not. Such facts would have only made Tien tasty Cabinet fodder at a Senate confirmation hearing. If only he could have boasted a Ming Na-Wen connection. Clinton likes her.

Of course, the White House denied there was any connection. But this is hardball politics.

What's more pathetic is that Asian Americans don't know how to respond to any of this AC/DC stuff.

We're freaked out. Is racism involved? Is this about America's fear of foreigners? Is it all just about money? Yes, yes, yes.

But, we can't respond until we know where exactly we fit in as a community. And that's the problem. The whole AC/DC issue goes to the core of defining what we are, and what we aren't. We think we have a nice little umbrella called "Asian America" that puts us all together and boosts our numbers. But the AC/DC affair is telling us something about what we've become. And it's not what we thought.

Despite generations in America, we have yet to develop a lasting American sense of ourselves. We're still primarily Asians in America, rather than Asian Americans.

What do I mean? We still think Asian. Not American. And when we play American games, like politics, though we try to emulate Americans, we're still Asian.

Part of it is due to the fact that we remain a predominately immigrant community. In fact, the boom in immigration the last 30 years has created a community that doesn't know itself. There are immigrants from the '90s who can't relate with the more assimilated immigrants from the '60s. At least they both have accents and a connection to the home country. Sweet relatability.

The real split is between the aforementioned and second- and third-generation types. They're the more assimilated, American-born Asians who alternately find and lose their roots based on need. They're what I call the Situational Asians, who say "Cabinet post? I must be Asian."

On top of that, we have fourth- and fifth-generation members, some who no longer see themselves as Asians, period.

For convenience, I like to separate us all into two primary groups. The first is the Suburban Upwardly Mobile Assimilated Asians (SUMAs). They make up our traditional leaders—the doctors, lawyers, and professional classes. A mix between Republican and Democrat, they're mostly American born.

And then there's the Newly Arrived Naturalized Asians (NANAs), post-'60s immigrants from any Asian country, with or without money. According to exit polls after the last elections, NANAs leaned more Democrat. But in reality, they're just one step from the mother country. They're closer to it than they are to their community here.

So here's the scenario: Due to immigration, the SUMAs are now overrun by the NANAs. We're much more NANA than we want to think. Meanwhile, the SUMAs in their assimilation have become both more selfish and alienated. Community? Who needs it. That's why the NANAs are taking over. And when they try to talk money and power, and attempt to emulate SUMA success, there's only one way to trump a rich lawyer's or doctor's money. Get a bunch of rich Asian financiers on your side.

Suddenly, the NANA is a somebody. Do you think that wasn't a motivating factor for John Huang in bringing in the Lippo folks? Or for Charles Yah Lin Trie in bringing in the gun king? How about Johnny Chung and his beer baron? Unfortunately, they're all finding that standing on Asian money is a precarious way to gain stature in American politics.

Lacking an American sense of self, Asian American political players have also bypassed advocating for real community needs among U.S. policy-makers. That's old style, New Deal stuff. This is the '90s. Seduced by money and power, our new emerging NANA politicos have a new constituency and a new role. They are hell-bent on the fast track—as middlemen in U.S. politics for Asian interests.

That's why there's been no united stand by the community in the AC/DC affair.

East or West, we don't know which way to go.

December 27, 1996

The Price of Admission

There is "Asian bashing" and then there is "Asian bashing." One type can be more psychological, the other physical. Both are definitely instances of discrimination that hurt like hell.

I learned the difference between the two at the recent Asian American Journalists Convention. It's premiere plenary session, "The Price of Asian Political Involvement" featured three reporters—Josh Goldstein of the *Philadelphia Inquirer*, K. Connie Kang of the *Los Angeles Times*, and Owen Ullmann, of *Business Week*— all of whom have covered the Asian Campaign Donation Controversy, what I fondly call our community's AC/DC problem.

Joining them were Professor Alan Watanabe of the University of Massachusetts/Institute of Asian American Studies, and Francey Lim Youngberg, a savvy Filipina who is Executive Director of the Congressional Asian

Pacific American Caucus Institute (CAPACI).

The panel, carried on C-SPAN, discussed whether the contribution story had gone "off the track" and tended to single out Asian Americans. Professor Watanabe and Youngberg agreed that it did. Youngberg, in particular, was quick to point out that there is no desire on the community's part to blindly defend the men and women suspected of funneling illegal or improper contributions.

Predictably, the reporters were quick to defend the story as legitimate, though they admitted that some reports had gone too far.

Was it "Asian Bashing?"

"I don't want to call it 'Asian bashing,' because that's a loaded term," said Kang, a Korean American. "But covering this issue has been very educational for mainstream reporters who don't have a background in the Asian community."

I'll say. In fact, the mainstream has gone from total ignorance to total paranoia. When William Safire in the *New York Times* can jump from campaign finance to speculation of foreign espionage by China, the mainstream has taken to flailing its big stick in the dark. Only when Sen. Fred Thompson admitted recently that there may never be "a smoking gun" found on any espionage link have rabid partisans like Safire wiped the foam from their lips.

Still, the coverage has often been brutal with examples of caricature and language conjuring images of buckteeth, slanted eyes and coolie hats. Still have trouble with the term "Asian Bashing?" Check out the bruises. Asian Americans have been called up and questioned by investigators because their Asian names suddenly make them suspect. Qualified Asian Americans have been passed over for key government jobs out of fear that their names and appearance link them to the scandal.

And if there is any doubt Asian Americans have been given "special" treatment, witness the coverage in the recent story of one Thomas Kramer, German national. As I pointed out to the panel, while Congress spends $5 million to figure out how $3 million was donated, while it looks for something rotten in Asia, there has been some "real" news to sate the taste of the most ardent of those half-heartedly for campaign finance reform. Just last month, the Federal Election Commission (FEC) fined Thomas Kramer more than $300,000 dollars, the largest fine ever assessed to a foreign national for improper contributions.

My question for the panel: "Why was he spared the 'Asian Treatment'?"

Josh Goldstein of the *Philadelphia Inquirer* could only hem and haw, mildly defend his mainstream brethren and then admit it was just a matter of "timing."

Timing? Racist coverage is a matter of timing? And I guess the slaves just happened to be in the wrong century at the wrong time.

The Kramer story broke on Friday, and was buried in the papers on Saturday. This was a real story, about a man who gave both to the Democrats and Republicans, which resulted in the largest fine ever to a foreign national. This was like throwing a large cadaver to the media. At last, news! So where was Safire? What? No "Kraut-gate?" No "German-gate?" Why weren't all German names given the once over on donor lists? Why was Mr. Kramer, being blonde and blue-eyed, a white man, and all Germans in America given a free pass by the media?

"By the time I mentioned it to my editors, there was already an AP story," Goldstein said.

Which means, it was old, move on. Stick to the "big story." The Asians.

Was the decision by the mostly white mainstream editors intentionally racist?

"No," said Ullman, "But was it subconsciously so? Who knows?"

Perhaps the Asian story is just sexier to the media, with its possible links to Clinton. But the Kramer story proves that the media is selective. "Biased" is another word one can use. The media carnivores didn't want German meat. Who wants frankfurters when you can get Asian meat, pounded flat, chopped, diced, and stir-fried?

August 22, 1997

The Senate's Big Bash
Speaking Chinglish at the campaign-finance hearings

The media knows how to bash Asians. But the Senate? Who'd have thunk it?

We know what the media can do with a few Asians. We've seen it over and over since last November when the Asian Campaign Donation Controversy—our AC/DC problem—began.

The media was the source for such enlightening linguistic mergers such as "Indo-gate," which slammed the Indonesian Riady's. The built-in guilt by association offered by the marriage of anything Asian with the suffix "gate" was just too intriguing for word smiths. So racist editors came up with "China-gate," for all the allegations about foreign spies infiltrating our political system. And then they came up with "Lippo-gate," in reference to the Lippo conglomerate from Indonesia, allegedly involved in funneling money through the former Democratic National Committee fund-raiser and ex-Lippo employee John Huang. At least we were spared "Huang-gate."

The media has caught itself on the gate-crap, however. Editors have retreated to the more generic "Donor-gate." Perhaps this came about when Democratic contributor Robert Meyerhoff's name recently came up in the ongoing saga, and someone finally became sensitive at the offense of a headline that was some form of race-gate. One can only imagine the uproar over a "Jew-gate."

Still, no such retreat shall wipe from memory my pick for the media's most grievous sin: the image of James Riady's sinister black and white photo on the cover of *Newsweek*. It was like an international wanted sign posted at newsstands everywhere, transforming Riady into public enemy #1, the villainous political contributor from the East.

We've come to expect bruises from the media. Bashing sells newspapers and magazines. But were we prepared for the institutional bashing from the Senate?

Asian Americans had hoped the Senate would be more even-handed. After all, they're elected officials. Someday, they may need our votes and our money.

Boy, were we wrong.

As we entered week two of the Senate campaign finance hearings, there was Sen. Sam Brownback (R-Kansas) questioning former Democratic Finance Director Richard Sullivan about the compensation of John Huang. Besides being a key figure in the investigation, Huang is a naturalized American and a graduate of the University of Connecticut.

Sullivan explained to Sen. Brownback that Huang would receive more money "if things worked out."

Responded Sen. Brownback: "So no raise, no get bonus."

Students of the English language will note the Senator's abnormal sentence structure. Many might see the sentence as an attempt at some form of Asian ebonics, or Asi-onics. Most of us would see it simply as a racist remark.

If Brownback isn't Asian bashing, he sure let his stick show. Call it the "Utter from the gutter." At least, he didn't stick out his teeth and squint his eyes. Someone please tell Sen. Brownback that the hearings are on C-SPAN. And while you're at it, mention that he's not in Kansas anymore.

Brownback did make a half-hearted attempt at an apology. He could have come clean and admitted he was only mimicking Jerry Lewis's caricature of Asians, so dear to his heart. Sad that they're the only Asian images he has in his brain. Say "Asian" and the man thinks of Jerry Lewis or John Huang, the Fu Manchu of campaign finance. Imagine the world if the only white people Asians thought of were Jed Clampett and the Steve Martin character in *The Jerk*.

The Senator could have been honest and said, "I have a lot of deep-rooted cultural misunderstandings." A decent press secretary could have written him a prepared statement like that. And then we could have chalked it all up to the intelligence deficit of some white Americans. But there was no such admission. All he could muster was that he intended "no slight by my statement."

A lot of good that does for the wounds he opened. He didn't even offer a "Free Dim Sum Day" in the state of Kansas sometime after the hearings.

But wait, the cloud has a silver lining. As bad as the remark was, it couldn't have been better timed.

That very morning, the *Washington Post* had published a warning shot to all good sensitive souls who'd rather think for themselves. Essentially, the *Post* was shaking its big, bad nasty finger at any of us who would dare use Asian bashing as a defense for old John Huang.

In a snotty, unsigned editorial, the white conscience of

the *Post* writes: "There is another kind of immunity being sought on (Huang's) behalf by his friends and backers. It is a kind of immunity by reason of his ethnic background. ...The immunity it is meant to afford comes from presumably shaming those who are pursuing Mr. Huang's alleged violations of the law suggesting that they are acting out of a racial bias, not a desire to get to the bottom of the scandal. ... It is not 'racist,' 'Asian Bashing,' or any such loathsome practice to seek vigorously to find out the truth..."

Whoa!

Was that a pre-emptive strike to excuse the racism that would be exposed in the hearts of good Senators like Mr. Brownback of Kansas? Was his vigorous portrayal of Asians a truth-gathering technique? What's next? A Ouija board?

Or was the *Post* just attempting to say that Asian Americans were overstepping our bounds in calling for fair and equal treatment before the law?

No one in the community has suggested Mr. Huang be given a free pass on the basis of his DNA. His "Asianness" was not an issue, until Brownback's "utter from the gutter."

Asian Americans, perhaps more than any group outside the GOP, have been awaiting the hearings as the place where once and for all the truth could be found—free from the marketplace frenzy of the media, where innuendo turns to smoking gun and accusatory stories become executions. We'd hope a bi-partisan look may expose the fact that Asian Americans' alleged campaign crimes seem like hand-picked small potatoes compared to the millions given by corporations to influence and corrupt legislators.

In fact, many Asian Americans would just as soon hang Huang if he did anything wrong. So let the hearings provide the proof.

But Sen. Thompson, with Watergate glory on his mind, seems to be after the president more than the truth. He himself admitted last Sunday on NBC's *Meet the Press*, that there may never be any proof to link contributions to foreign governments.

No proof? No wonder all the GOP Senators seemed stoked on the subtext, openly expressed by Sen. Brownback: It's those foreigners again.

Without solid evidence, the Senate's no better than the media. What else can they do but bash and flail?

July 18, 1997

11

Political Winds

IN POLITICS THESE DAYS, one must use the phrase "thar she blows" advisedly. Someone may take you literally.

Monica Lewinsky did.

Some people say the Clinton scandal is more than sex. That it's about lies and perjury and a president being above the law. But all that seems besides the point. It's still about sex.

Asian Americans don't seem to be too upset about the whole thing. As my friend Mei-ling Sze, the news anchor and managing editor of the Cantonese Evening News, says, "Asians are very practical people, who want leaders to take care of crime, education and the economy. They're used to the Emperor having 300 wives."

But Kenneth Starr cares. In Clinton's video taped testimony, Starr constantly badgered the president over definitions of sex. It's the kind of thing that would drive one to have sex with a badger.

Which would be okay, since that would not have been under the definition of sex in the Paula Jones case.

If you watched the Clinton testimony the first time focused on Clinton, consider instead the off-camera Independent Counsel and his deputies. Unseen, moralistic, powerful enough to un-do the last two presidential elections. Listen to their "sex police-type" questions, and the president's answers, and tell me who is the greater threat to our democracy?

Rules of the Game
Lessons from the White House

State of the Union? Middle East? Saddam Hussein? Yes, there are many hot issues in the world today, but I'm pleased to say the media has put the really silly stuff on hold in order to focus on far juicier matters. In other words, "We interrupt this presidency to bring you something really sordid about high people in low places."

Call it "Clinton Interuptus."

Every day there's something new. Here are just a few things I've learned this past week:

1. If you cheat, you will get caught. This is a truism that needs to be tested only among the most suicidal of persons. In the case of the President, I'll take him at his word that he did not have improper sexual relations. I just don't find it necessary to check for the absence of bite marks on the Presidential equipment. Not at this time.

But the fact that Mr. Clinton is going through a "crisis" at the moment proves that it really doesn't matter if anyone has the "goods" on you when it comes to hanky-panky, presidential or otherwise. You're going to have a problem. Any practitioner of the extra-marital goes through an extremely difficult period of "explaining." This could be, at the very least, mildly distracting for a head of state. For example, I'd find it problematic if, while worrying about Saddam Hussein's cache of biological weapons, the President wondered if it included a spermicide.

2. You will get caught if anyone you do it with knows anyone named Tripp. It's clear now that the number one question to ask anyone who might qualify for a presidential "sortie" is: "Do you know, or have you ever

known Linda Tripp?"

Tripp is the woman with a soft shoulder to cry on and a microphone in her brassiere. That's a dead give away. Never trust a woman who has a microphone in brassiere. She's the kind of friend you don't need: a woman with an agenda, who, just as you start to cry and get emotional, asks, "Can you take that again from the top, but this time with a little less mucus?"

She was so upset about being portrayed as a liar by Clinton's lawyer that she combined her political vendetta ("You do know, Vincent Foster was murdered by the left, right?") with a personal one ("Bill Clinton is an amoral dog."). Tripp was the one who not only taped Monica Lewinsky, she outed another allegedly fondled woman, Kathleen Willey. All in the name of our unfondled Republic. Neither Lewinsky nor Willey was in a necessarily complaining mood. But Tripp sure was.

I find it troubling that while Clinton and Lewinsky remain the focus, Tripp is seen as a kind of sexual Paul Revere. "The interns are coming! The interns are coming!" If she succeeds in bringing down the chief executive officer of the land, is she the true patriot? Does she become "Ms. Wired for the Prosecution," the most moral avenger of all? Or does she remain the selfish, venal, and petty bureaucrat she is?

It's sad, because don't you think the Super Bowl would have been even more memorable this year if the sight of John Elway's teeth didn't constantly remind us of Monica Lewinsky's overbite?

It all could have been avoided with some simple vetting. If only the President knew what he was really looking for: Tripp-less sex.

What bothers me is having a president who may not have taken his sexual appointees with the same seriousness as his political non-sexual appointees. After all the President puts potential cabinet members through, you'd think he'd be more careful about the nominees for that special trip to the Supine, er, Oval Office. Just look at the ringer our dear friend Bill Lann Lee went through for an office down the road at the Justice Department as the "acting" head of the Civil Rights Division.

3. There's still nothing like s-e-x. Oh, money comes close. But money doesn't have the subtext sex does. That's because greed is basically OK in capitalist America. Money? Take all you want. Sex? Don't take all you want. There are limits to good taste. You want to get AIDS? And while you're at it, use a condom, for goodness sakes. That's why sex sells. We repress it so much that when it's dangled in front of us, we've got to have it. Now. That's why we can't get enough of the White House scandal. We're repulsed and attracted to it all at the same time. We say our interest is high-minded and legal. We say we're concerned with "suborning perjury." But it's really about s-e-x.

We're like the people in Congress who like to investigate pornography. Oh how they hate it. And oh, how they can't get enough of it. Notice how the best investigations never come to an end. They're on-going. Theye've become a noveau Victorian society. Hung up. Clinton on the other hand is "Clintonesque." Merely hung. Full of himself. The young conqueror stud. At some point, you'd figure the two forces would butt heads.

But it all makes me wonder if John Huang isn't thanking his Chinese Moons that he repressed his sexual urges. In all of last year's campaign finance scandal there was talk of big business and money. There was espionage even. But no sex.

It's made all the difference. After causing a panic

attack among some conservatives, Huang has disappeared from Scandalville.

I had thought that xenophobia was enough to make the issue of campaign finance an important story. Xenophobia is always a nice race wedge and it does contain an "x." But no, fear of foreigners was not enough to raise the ire of the American public to anything approaching our Lewinsky tale. Change the campaign-finance laws? Hey we've got to change the White House intern-application process first!

Imagine if Sen. Fred Thompson had found geisha girls instead of Buddhist nuns! No smoking gun? Howabout smoking condoms! Washington would have been orgasmic over changing the finance laws.

What did we get instead? Charlie Trie shaking Hillary's hand? You call that "presidential touching?" Johnny Chung "stalking" the First Lady to goose his fax business? Ooh. I'm titillated.

Sex indeed was the missing factor. Think how much money John Huang could have raised if he had set up a simple 900 number with the President for phone sex. Or he could have just gone around with a sign. "Live Sex Talk with President—$25,000."

What a missed opportunity. And to think, Asians were still treated like yesterday's bean sprouts.

Finally, let's all be thankful that when I saw Mr. Clinton leering at actress Ming Na Wen at the Congressional Asian Pacific American Caucus Institute dinner a few years back, he was merely feigning a taste for Asian women.

Better Monica Lewinsky than Monica Lew, don't you think? If not for the nation, then for the community.

January 29, 1998

Yellow Bean Counting
Dueling exit poll data for Election '96

Well, what did you do behind the drawn curtains? Who'd you vote for? What did you vote for?

That's the question nosy Asian Pacific Americans are wondering after Election Day 1996, one that no doubt was the most exit-polled election to date of Asian Pacific Americans. Frankly, I don't know if there's really any way of knowing how someone voted. Not unless you're a spouse, a sibling, or a lover. These are exit polls, mind you. People do lie, though perhaps in some circumstances an exit poller may have a better shot at the truth than a spouse. Alas, we live in an imperfect world, and must make do. Unfortunately, the exit polls of Asian Americans in 1996 show results as different as day and night.

So what did you do when the curtains were drawn? Who'd you vote for? What did you vote for?

Well, just as a piano has the white keys and the dark keys, which numbers do you want? The white ones or the yellow ones?

White Numbers: This year ABC, CBS, NBC, CNN, Fox, AP—essentially the white ethnic media—ganged up and pooled their immense and unlimited resources to hire Voter News Service (VNS) as the official voice of mainstream America. These would be the most widely reported numbers in the country. And here's the beauty of it all—no one will be wrong. They'd all be reporting the same thing! Talk about a godsend to a news exec. This is like using the pool camera for the O.J. trial. The only thing you can screw up is the spin.

VNS interviewed 15,873 voters and came up with these representative numbers for Asian Americans in the nation: 49 percent of you went for the loser, Bob

Dole. I guess some people just chose to close their eyes to Dole's anti-immigrant, anti-affirmative action, pro-English only stance.

The VNS poll showed 42 percent of Asian Americans voted for the winner, President Bill Clinton. I suppose that's to be expected when your biggest Asian American supporters are either wealthy noncitizens or nonvoting, meditating Buddhist monks.

Eight percent of Asian Americans in the VNS exit poll said they were Perot voters. I believe the same voters were said to have picked up Radio Beijing signals on their Toshiba rice cookers.

So here's the mainstream version of Asian Americans in Campaign '96: 49 percent Dole, 42 percent Clinton, eight percent Perot. The overall popular vote nationwide was 41 Dole, 49 Clinton, nine percent Perot. Asian Americans are practically the exact opposites on the major candidates. Far less Clinton-ish, John Huang notwithstanding. And significantly, far more Dole-ish. Whites were 45 percent Dole. Are Asian Americans whiter than white? Well, for sure, we're just as paranoid about Perot.

Those are the widely reported numbers that jibe with the notion that Asian Americans are somewhat conservative. Even President Clinton acknowledged that at his post-election White House news conference as he referred to the John Huang affair. "There has been a lot of rather disparaging comments made about Asian Americans," Clinton said. "And .... ironically, I found it surprising that our friends on the other side did because, historically, they have received more votes from Asian Americans than we have."

But did that really happen in 1996?

This year a number of Asian American groups did their own thing. And why not? Generally, mainstream polls rely on only a small sample of Asian Americans. It's one reason why mainstream polls are notorious for just giving results in terms of race in simplified terms. There's white. There's black. That's it. For example, national sex studies would lead you to believe Asians don't have sex.

More significant than our sexual habits, however, are our language skills. The issue of English proficiency and the issuance of bilingual election material remain the greatest barriers to APA participation. If such care is needed in the official polling booth, shouldn't it be required outside in the un-official "official" exit polls in order to get a true picture of what's happening?

The fact is English-only exit polls assure results primarily of mainstream English-speaking APAs. When the community is up to two-thirds immigrant, can mainstream polls ever see what's below the surface?

Yellow Numbers: This year the Asian Pacific American legal groups in the major population hubs of mainland Asian America (N.Y., L.A., S.F.-Oakland) took it upon themselves to conduct their own nonpartisan exit polls. Furthermore, they went a step beyond. In Southern California, 950 APAs were polled; 53 percent of them asked for and completed an exit questionnaire in an Asian language.

Remember those Dole-ish numbers of VNS? In Los Angeles County, which constitutes the largest APA electorate in the U.S., the Asian Pacific American Legal Center of Southern California found 61 percent of APAs voted Clinton, 32 percent Dole, six percent Perot. All APA groups with the exception of Vietnamese voted for Clinton in higher than expected proportions. Clinton received 65 percent of the Chinese American vote, 60 percent of the Korean American vote, 56 percent of the Japanese American vote, and 51 percent of the Filipino

American vote; 49 percent of Vietnamese Americans voted Clinton.

In the San Francisco-Oakland area, the Asian Law Caucus conducted a similar poll of 500 APAs. It reported that 83 percent voted for Clinton, just nine percent for Dole. Half of the Chinese-American voters requested a bilingual exit-poll questionnaire.

In New York, the Asian American Legal Defense and Education Fund conducted a poll of 3,200 APAs. Seventy-one percent voted for Clinton, 21 percent for Dole.

They all show the same trends: extremely high voter turnout among APAs, a large concentration of first-time voters (up to a third in the Southern California poll), and an immigrant community of both newcomers and more assimilated APAs that is much more Democrat and pro-Clinton than the general public is led to believe. Skewed picture? How could it be? The community polls actually talked to real Asians.

As for the discrepancy between the yellow numbers and the white numbers, I think it's clearly the cultural and language barrier. But what might be more interesting is where the mainstream and the culturally sensitive meet.

On the issue of Prop. 209, Californians voted yes to end state-run affirmative action, 54 percent to 48 percent. The VNS poll, however, showed that Asian Americans went against the mainstream: 45 percent of Asian Americans voted yes on 209, 55 percent voted no—a majority of Asian Americans.

An overwhelming majority? No, just whelming. The community polls show overwhelming. In the Southern California poll, 76 percent of APAs voted no. In S.F.-Oakland, 84 percent voted no.

For Election Day 1996, the bottom line for Asian Americans seems to be this: Between the Suburban

Upwardly Mobile Assimilated Asians (SUMAs) who found their way to the mainstream exit polls and lean Republican, and the Newly Arrived Naturalized Asians (NANAs) who found their way to the community exit polls and surprisingly lean more Democratic, our communities come together when we feel the sting of discrimination. As the folks at Texaco know, just when you think you belong, someone points out you're just a yellow jelly bean.

November 15, 1996

Asian Smoke Screen
Where Big Tobacco is headed next

For some time now tobacco companies have been involved in a marketing push that could qualify as a new definition for genocide.

As domestic anti-smoking battles continue, American companies have been increasingly looking abroad for new smokers—specifically, Third World Asian countries. The reality is, for every dead American smoker looking for a grave, Big Tobacco's replacing him with a handful of young, soon-to-be-addicted Asian smokers. But it's seen as a foreign-trade issue, not a health and moral issue. A smoke screen, for sure. So you won't hear much about it in the aftermath of the Big Tobacco settlement. Not even if someone tracks the number of Asian immigrants who come to America with their American-supported nasty habits.

That's why, when the big accord was announced last week, there was a strange euphoria. The state attorneys general and the law firms representing Big Tobacco seemed to be smiling so much, you'd think they were in bed together. It's funny they didn't light up a smoke afterward in honor of their backroom legal tryst. Was it good for you? It sure was good for both of them.

To toss out more than 40 lawsuits and 17 class-action suits, the states got the tobacco companies to pay $368.5 billion in the first 25 years, and then $15 billion a year thereafter. (California is due more than $1 billion for MediCal payments and business penalties.) For this, the tobacco companies paid the highest legal fees in history. Their attorneys took home $2 billion for their time and effort. Of course, if you're a tobacco company guy, you can't go around admitting how good this all feels, especially since it's common knowledge that $2 billion paid to a hooker would probably feel better.

No, a happy tobacco official would only appear to be gloating unnecessarily. So it would only be proper that any Big Tobacco exec appear contrite and glum in public, even though they'd have a right to gloat. Paying $2 billion to your lawyers to stabilize the base of a multibillion-dollar industry, well, that's more than just a good business deal. That's a real coup.

But what about the settlement's imposed restrictions on tobacco marketing and advertising? What about all the mandated anti-smoking messages? And then there's that $368.5 billion? Won't that hurt the tobacco companies?

Somewhere out there in Tobacco Land, you're hearing something in the air. But it's probably not, "Ouch." More than likely it's some tobacco heiress singing, "Don't Cry For Me Raleigh-Durham." The truth is the agreement doesn't make the kind of dent on the tobacco business that we were all led to believe. No matter how stringent a domestic settlement may sound, tobacco's future is not America, but rather Asia, where the spread of death by cigarettes continues unfettered.

After the settlement, one attorney general may have

proclaimed in glee, "The Marlboro Man will be riding into the sunset on Joe Camel." He may be, but the grizzled cowpuncher is almost certainly rising in the East, bigger and stronger than ever, riding roughshod over a new group of increasingly addicted people. Generally speaking, they're all Asian, an effort that one anti-smoking activist called a renewal of the Opium Wars.

The numbers tell the story. Tobacco companies are drooling over Asia's Third World countries because that's where the smokers are. In developed countries like the U.S., the World Health Organization estimates that a mere 300 million people smoke. That figure more than doubles in developing countries, where the number of smokers exceeds 800 million.

Tobacco companies have long seen the writing on the wall. For years, exports have been the answer to smoking's decline at home. Traditionally, Western Europe and Latin America have been the focus, adding roughly $4 billion a year in profits to tobacco companies. But in the last 15 years the new mass market is Asia—notably Thailand, Taiwan, Japan, South Korea, and China, where there are 300 million smokers alone.

In the past, the Asian state-run monopolies have hampered the efforts of U.S. tobacco to take a foothold. And though state-run monopolies sound pretty horrible themselves, they have emerged as a kind of lesser of two evils. The state-run firms tend to make inferior products and have terrible marketing plans. Smoking is seen as unattractive as it really is. Fewer people tend to smoke. Consequently, fewer tend to die from cigarette-related illness.

But Big Tobacco has been smart. While fighting the government over smoking domestically, it's enlisted a big ally to boost foreign sales: the U.S. government.

You might call it "Operation: Give Me Liberty, Give Me

Cigarettes." With help especially from the Reagan and Bush administrations, it's helped the companies rack up larger profits than ever before.

Last fall, the *Washington Post* documented just how chummy government has been with the tobacco companies. A January 1986 memo from George Griffin, commercial counselor at the U.S. embassy in Seoul, to Matthew Winokur, public affairs manager of Philip Morris, Grifin spells out the relationship: "No matter how this process spins itself out, I want to emphasize that the embassy and various U.S. government agencies in Washington will keep the interests of Philip Morris and the other American cigarette manufacturers in the forefront of our daily concerns."

The government's biggest battering ram has been its bullyish use of Section 301 of the 1974 Trade Act. It allowed for the U.S. trade representative not only to investigate unfair trade practices, but enabled Washington to invoke retaliatory sanctions against countries. It worked like magic against Japan. By September 1986, with Section 301 retaliation documents set to go to the president, Nakasone gave in to the pressure.

Today American cigarette exports are 21 percent of the Japanese market and earn $7 billion in annual sales. Female smoking is at an all-time high, and female college freshmen are four times more likely to smoke than their mothers. One by one, Asian countries have opened up to American tobacco. In 1994, almost 700 billion cigarettes were sold outside the United States. So far, China has been the most resistant monopoly, but American companies have a three percent share and spend more than 40 million in advertising there already. Who knows what could happen if China loosens up? You may even be able to ban cigarettes in America. The tobacco companies won't care. The cash flow will be there. But so will the death flow.

Epidemiologist Richard Peto of Oxford University says worldwide smoking deaths number three million per year. In China alone, 50 million who are currently 18 or younger will eventually die from smoking-related disease. As Clinton and Congress scrutinize the tobacco pact, the Asian factor shouldn't be dismissed. Until it's addressed, any punitive measure against Big Tobacco is a slap on the wrist. The exporting of death remains a loophole for American companies, a giant-sized smoke ring.

June 27, 1997

Political Ambitions
'Acting' like we've triumphed

Asian Americans and Bill Lann Lee got an early Christmas gift this week when Lee was named the acting assistant attorney general for civil rights by President Clinton. This is not to be confused with the job of "assistant attorney general for civil rights in acting," a position devoted to the assurance that a white man will never again play the role of Charlie Chan.

But there is some acting involved here.

Asian Americans will have to act like this is a great triumph. We'll have to act like this is better than nothing at all. And it is marginally.

As acting assistant attorney general for civil rights, Lee is literally placed in a role that should last him through Clinton's term. Use of the term "acting" was a necessary political maneuver because of the GOP roadblock of the confirmation process. The Republicans insisted that Lee was a quota-monger, a left-wing ideologue, never mind his past displays of fairness and equanimity under the law. How do you get an 800-pound elephant named Orrin Hatch to get out of the way? Not easily. The term acting moved the elephant and allowed Republicans to save face. But exactly what kind of face does it leave for Bill Lann Lee?

Sure he gets the job, but once again an Asian American, a person of color, is made to feel less than welcome in a premier career post. The president has said that he will resubmit Lee's name and hope for full confirmation. Even Asian American political advocates are gearing up to continue the fight for Bill Lann Lee. They know that this week's appointment makes it very clear that Lee enters his position without the full title or authority to do the job.

Keep in mind it could be worse. He could be a "lame duck." They're the ones that end up hanging from the neck in your local Chinatown delis.

But one becomes a lame duck only after first flapping onto the scene as a strong duck.

In Lee's case, he enters stage left—acting.

And I know what acting means. It means that Pierce Brosnan isn't James Bond. You want to kick his butt? Go ahead. He's acting. George Clooney isn't really Batman. Neither is he a doctor on TV. He's as much a doctor as Jenny McCarthy is a natural D cup.

That's acting for you.

In political terms, Ronald Reagan was an actor who was president. He may have been acting but we know he was never acting. He was voted in.

In Lee's case, one must wonder how others will see the term acting. What precisely will it mean to the people he encounters in the political world? Not good enough? Not white enough? Not conservative enough? Not powerful enough?

Here's the tragedy in this case. Bill Lann Lee is more than qualified for the position. He is better than good enough. He deserved it all. But the politics of the situation gave him less than he deserved. President Clinton was forced to do the right thing. He circumvented the Senate and made the appointment without approval, as is his right. It definitely passes the smell test. This was affirmative action at the highest level. It wasn't needed because of the person, but rather due to the poisonous political environment.

But what kind of message does all this maneuvering send?

To me, there are some simple lessons. For starters, merit doesn't really mean a thing. It's still a matter of who you know, who'll go to bat for you, and how much you'll settle for. If you're a qualified Asian American like Lee, or a person of color who doesn't meet some Republican ideological quota, you'll have to settle for less. Much less. But don't worry. Act happy.

December 18, 1997

12

Food Fight

MY WIFE, KATHY, is an animal rights activist. Not some weekend prankster, but a real committed, life-long, 100 percent animal rights activist. It's her career.

Some people think I became a vegetarian so that she would have sex with me. That is only partially true.

It seemed like a fair deal. She took my name. I took on some of her beliefs.

What is true is that being married to an animal rights activist makes you question certain things in life that you would otherwise ignore. Like the life taken by the fresh-kill butchers in the Chinatown markets, or the images of carcasses hanging in Asian markets throughout the country.

It was gradual for me at the start. I was a selfish vegetarian. I did it because I didn't want to have a lard-encased pulmonary artery. But slowly I saw that the attitude toward the pigs and the chickens was no different from the attitudes I saw among humans. Put yourself in the hooves and talons of a pig or chicken and experience the pain of discrimination. You may not get eaten literally, but figuratively we've all been devoured, digested, and expelled just because we were silent, voiceless, and the wrong color.

When you view racism through a less anthropomorphic lens, you might begin to think twice about that pork chop or T-bone steak. And you can't make it taste better with a little soy sauce and garlic.

We're Animals Too

One argument for vegetarianism

As a simple matter of wearing my compassion in my lead, let me say up-front that no animals were harmed in the writing of this column—unless you include editors.

Now that we've cleared that up, I am pleased to note that this Sunday marks the event known as the March for the Animals in Washington, D.C., the centerpiece of World Animal Awareness Week. Thousands of people are expected to march on the capitol. I would hope that there would be many Asian Pacific Americans joining in. Maybe a latter-day Gandhi or two. Unfortunately, I doubt many APAs will be there. And that will be a real shame. I mean, after all, we're animals too.

In fact, I wonder if members of APA groups or other minorities will even take the issue seriously enough to pay attention and show up. I don't expect many will.

One of the sad truths and dirty little secrets about the animal rights movement has been its failure to outreach Asian Americans, Hispanics, and African Americans. Without that, the animal-rights movement remains a predominantly white, middle-class, mostly female affair. Talk about the need for diversity. It's one movement that could stand a little affirmative action. Anything less would debilitate a movement in this country where the Census Bureau projects "minorities" will become the majority by the year 2050.

So, animal-rights types have no excuse. What's our excuse? We're too busy to notice. We've got our own tails to worry about. Civil rights. Gender rights. Human rights. Where do you fit animal rights? In between lunch and dinner? Or perhaps as lunch and dinner? We're humans; we should come first, right?

Wrong.

What people fail to see is that all rights are basically intertwined. For example, the civil-rights movement took root as a response to the remnants of slavery, a practice that was justified because blacks were seen as less than human, as animals to be used and exploited. It's the only way to justify discrimination, or any kind of substandard treatment. You can only treat someone like dirt after you've convinced yourself they're less than human, merely animals, unworthy of equal standing to the "master." All minorities in this country, at some point in history, have faced that kind of treatment.

In these times, as minorities form coalitions seeking recognition, respect, and empowerment in society, it seems odd that we lose sight of how all discrimination comes from the same self-centered seed. Minorities and animals are fighting the same irrational instinct, the "master's instinct" to dominate and exploit. To that degree we are allied, and a fight by compassionate activists on behalf of voiceless animals is no more absurd than a fight on behalf of a voiceless people.

That's why it seems odd to me that more minorities don't embrace animal rights as a fundamental part of their own fight for equality. More than 25 million animals are killed annually in labs in the U.S. Many die in the name of products such as those made by Procter & Gamble and Johnson & Johnson. With the growing number of companies that sell cruelty-free products, clearly, there is no need to exploit animals for cosmetics testing.

But it's also time to consider ending the use of animals in medical research. The animal model is an imperfect one that all too often misleads researchers. As an example, aspirin causes birth defects in rats, mice, and monkeys—but not in humans. Arsenic causes cancer in humans, but not in rats. Animals can't tell us how they feel. Rats can't even vomit. The animal model wastes money and time, and essentially does little more than provide a multimillion-dollar welfare system to scientists. The future of research lies in the use of non-animal tests, such as epidemiological studies.

Of course, you'll hear the research establishment use AIDS activists like Jeff Getty to show that animal rights activists are impeding progress. Nothing could be further from the truth. Using animals only prolongs research—it's a red herring. It doesn't find a cure. It works only toward the preservation of a cruel, exploitative view of animals.

Yet all too often, even those of us who have felt exploitation ourselves have come to accept the master's view of the world just fine when it comes to animals. I mean, we're human. A pig is an animal. And *Babe* was just a movie. Let's eat. I used to take that view. Of course, after more of my family died of heart failure, I began to reconsider. I've always called myself a selfish vegetarian for that reason. I eat tofu because I don't want a heart attack. Before this week, I wouldn't have considered myself an ethical vegetarian, that is to say, a vegetarian concerned about an animal's pain. Those folks are fanatics, right?

But then I saw something the other day that changed my mind.

I was driving through Oakland's Chinatown, down 8th Street, and made a left turn on Webster, a street lined with restaurants and delis. The traffic was snarled by a double-parked panel truck, the size of a small moving van. It was an unmarked truck, except for a small notation by the license plate that indicated it belonged to a meat company. As drivers honked, the Asian driver, decked in butcher's sanitary whites, got out, went to the rear, and rolled up the back door, revealing what definitely was not an array of perfectly manicured ribs and chops. It was a truck packed tight like a sausage, loaded from floor to ceiling with bodies.

It was like an army truck coming in from the front line—except there were no body bags. It was just body, on top of body, on top of body. The bodies were long and lean. Like those of a 7-year-old, except they had no life. The life had been stripped away, and now the carcasses were stiffening, one on top of the other like bricks of flesh.

The bodies didn't move. But the faces remained expressive. They had eyes, all open, staring out into the street—at me in my car.

I kept thinking, "Holocaust," not to demean or trivialize the historical event, but just to make sense of such a sight. From ceiling to floor, wall to wall. Bodies, on top of bodies, on top of bodies.

Suddenly, they weren't just pigs anymore. They were victims.

June 21, 1996

No Time To Kill

Fresh kill practices must go

As a Filipino American, I know my countrymen are saddled with the "dog-eating" thing. But that's another column. For now, I just want you to know, at least we don't have the "cat-eating" thing. Unlike the Chinese who have both the "dog-eating" thing and the "cat-eating" thing. In China, cats are considered a delicacy—to eat. That's right. Cats. Just like that thing on your lap. Andrew Lloyd Webber. You know, *Memory*. OK, how about Garfield? They're for eating.

But have you thought about how hard it is to first get

193

the fur off the darn things? You'd have to get the fur off first. You wouldn't want it on your teeth. No toothpick could get that out.

A recent HBO documentary showed how they deal with cats at a typical Chinese market. First, they boil the water. Then they toss in the cat—alive. That loosens up the skin, and then they peel the cat like a ripe mango. Sometimes the cats aren't quite dead from the shock of boiling water. But, the workers have to meet demand. The parboiled cats—eyes opened, breathing—get skinned anyway. It's a tradition in China.

Fortunately, I haven't seen a cat trimmed down for hors d'oeuvres here in our local Chinatowns. But I can't say the same for the fish, frogs, crabs, turtles, and chickens, for whom abuse and torture is a common, everyday occurrence. It has been for years.

As a kid, I would accompany my Dad on the 30-minute bus ride into San Francisco's Chinatown just to shop. He was a Filipino cook after all, and you just couldn't get all the things you need back where I lived in the Mission district. Fresh tortillas, maybe. But, where else but Chinatown could he find those bumpy, monster-size bitter melons? Or all those weird greens that look like stuff in your back yard, only they tasted better when you had to pay for them.

Mostly, my father shopped for vegetables. But I would go with him to see the animals. The live fish in the small bowls. The chickens in their tiny cages. The turtles swimming in shallow pans. I wanted to take them all home as pets.

Then I realized, they weren't pets. They were dinner. They only killed the animals in Chinatown. You could smell it.

These days, the only thing I'd kill for in Chinatown is a parking place. I don't eat meat. Or seafood. And I don't shop in the markets. But, it certainly pleased me to no end to see San Francisco officials recently taking the markets to task over their fresh-kill practices.

The markets have had a free pass for too long.

The idea of a fish being butchered live before your very eyes—entrails flying, carcass wiggling—may stimulate some taste buds, but it offends me as brutal and callous.

To paraphrase an old saying, put yourself in the fish's fins and see how you like it. An Asian butcher, wielding a big cleaver, starts hacking away at you, and doesn't have the decency to give you an anesthetic first!

OK, how about a blindfold? Say you're a frog. You were happy sitting on your lily pad, when suddenly you're stuck in a bag and get the crap beat out of you. Not much better is it?

No, the only sane way is to ban fresh kill. Fresh kill is antiquated, unsanitary, and unnecessary.

And fresh kill is cruel. There are laws against that.

Of course, this has brought out fresh kill advocates to fight on behalf of turtle, frog, and fish torture.

"How far does this animal rights stuff go?" they ask. "What's next: plant rights?"

Well, if you can't tell the difference between a carp and a carrot, I can't help you. But, the fact of the matter is, plants can be considered endangered, and are therefore worthy of protection.

The real question for fresh kill advocates is "Why do they resist?" Would it be too much to sell an already dead fish?

No one is talking about markets not selling meat and fish. That would be wonderful, but one ideal situation at a time. At this point, fresh kill opponents merely want markets to follow laws concerning cruelty and sanitation.

But the markets continue their ways, as if there is something tasty in the kill. Balderdash. A *Los Angeles*

Times food critic did a study not long ago that proved that dead fish go through a remarkable change just like humans: rigor mortis. Surprisingly, the stiff dead fish actually produces a hormone that enhances its taste. This was corroborated by the critic, whose own taste test proved the natural superiority of the rigor mortis fish.

I'd hate to see all those fresh-kill advocates miss out on that taste treat!

So, if it's not taste, what else can they be getting riled up about. Culture? Tradition? Race?

No one has played those cards yet. But there have been hints. Every time a fresh kill advocate talks about how they've been doing this for ages, just as they did in the mother country, watch out. Any claim of cultural racism here would be a sad, divisive thing. And totally wrong.

Many Asians have had a long history of vegetarianism brought on by religion. Buddha didn't get fat on Big Macs.

Sadder still is to hear fresh-kill advocates mouth the same arguments that have been used for centuries to keep minorities in their place.

When someone says, "These aren't pets, they're just food," it echoes the same sentiments used to keep Asian Americans, blacks, and Hispanics in exploitable, subservient roles in society.

When someone says, "Animal rights? What's next, plants?" see how easily one can transpose that line to say any of the following: "Why should Filipinos become citizens? Next they'll make monkeys citizens." "Why should women vote? What's next, pigs?" "Why should blacks be free? What's next, mules?"

They're all arguments that have been used historically to uphold discrimination in America. Fresh killer logic honors the same tradition of exploitation. Fresh kill advocates are just too blind and too selfish to see it.

August 2, 1996

13

A Holiday Sampler

I ENJOY HOLIDAYS AS MUCH as the next guy. A day off is always welcome. But I often wonder if the meaning of the holidays gets lost. All holidays. Even American ones. Martin Luther King Day is one such day. It's a day that many Asians still don't understand. "I'm not black," they say, as they take the day off.

Heritage month is another great example. The only people who feel like taking it seriously are the guilty non-Asians. The rest don't seem to care that there's a month to celebrate "us."

Holidays are days of respect. They're not just an excuse for a party. Beyond consumption, it's a time for contemplation and tradition. That's why they come around just once a year.

Black and White and in Color
Why we need Heritage Month

I went up to the first Asian American guy I saw this month and gave him my standard greeting in May. I stuck out my hand, beamed, and said, loudly, "Hey, Happy Asian Pacific American Heritage Month!"

It was loud enough so that all the non-Asian types around me could experience it too. That's what the month is supposed to be about. Letting people know about us.

Instead, I learned about us. This man, an acquaintance, was caught totally by surprised. He's like a lot of Asian Americans in the Bay Area: bright, successful to a point, living in silent satisfaction. I figured maybe he thought I was a Spanish guy, with a name like Guillermo.

Still, his embarrassment over my greeting stunned me. A "Merry Christmas" he would've handled. Maybe even a "Happy Columbus Day." People respect Columbus. He gave them a day off. But a "Happy Asian Pacific American Heritage Month?" Forget it.

The man didn't mention anything more about it. Instead, he tried to pretend that I never even mentioned it. And then he gave me a look as if I had the "cooties" or something approximating mad cow disease. Or, since I'm vegetarian, a case of mad tofu. It's an amok derivative, whatever it is.

That has been my lone APA Heritage Month experience. There haven't been many for me this year. But I'm still trying to get in the spirit.

When I lived in Washington, D.C., there were heritage month experiences practically every minute of May.

It used to make me glad to see June come around. Now here we are, approaching Memorial Day, which may as well be in honor of what has been an utterly dead Asian

198

Pacific American Heritage Month.

Consider this sad state:

- Not one Hallmark card.
- Not one school program for which my daughter was asked to bring in lumpias.
- Not one public cultural program that featured hula dancing girls with coconut half-shell bikini tops.

And I don't think I heard the media exposing even one little known cultural fact about the Cambodian, Hmong, Laotian, Thai, Bangladeshi, Burmese, Indonesian, Malayan, Okinawan, Pakistani, Sri Lankan, Tongan, Tahitian, Northern Mariana Islander, Palauan, and Fijian. Not to mention, the Chinese, Filipino, Japanese, Asian Indian, Korean, Vietnamese, Hawaiian, Samoan, and Guamanian.

Maybe that's the problem. The guest list sounds more like a shotgun wedding. Celebrate our heritage?

Which one?

The name has always been a problem. Who calls themselves Asian Pacific American?

Hardly anybody.

I was recently speaking to a Filipino student group at the University of San Francisco when I asked that question. Who considers themselves Asian Pacific American or Asian American or Asian Pacific Islander? Not a single student raised a hand.

They called themselves "Filipino" flat out. Or "Filipino American." The troubling thing is that Filipinos, at 1,406,770 (according to the latest census), are the second largest group among Asian Pacific Americans and the largest group in California.

When a large group within the APA category doesn't identify with "Asian Pacific American," how do we expect non-Asians to figure it out?

It's really our unique problem. Politicians gave us the handle so they could identify us, categorize us, and find a bureaucratic way to address us. But while "Asian Pacific American" is the marquee of the big hotel that houses us, we prefer our separate rooms: Cambodian, Hmong, Laotian, Thai, Bangladeshi, Burmese, Indonesian, Malayan, Okinawan, Pakistani, Sri Lankan, Tongan, Tahitian, Northern Mariana Islander, Palauan, and Fijian. Not to mention, the Chinese, Filipino, Japanese, Asian Indian, Korean, Vietnamese, Hawaiian, Samoan, and Guamanian. Oh, and close the door behind you.

This is unfortunate since we need each other.

We may not like the strange phrase "Asian Pacific American," but we need it to bring us together. Whites didn't become the majority by insisting on being called Welsh American or Dutch American or Danish American. There are roughly 7.3 million Asian Pacific Americans, three percent of the U.S. population. We barely show up as it is. As individual groups we're like flies on a big horse. But all together, we might actually get to ride the horse. Just by uttering "Asian Pacific American," we evolve from fly to cowboy.

The Wild West is an apt metaphor for race in this country. Race will remain the hot-button issue for some time to come, partly because we are entering unexplored territory. How many people have really had to deal with the Hmong explosion?

Instead, we get a rehash of tried-and-true topics. For example, ABC just did a huge series on race during Asian Pacific American Heritage Month. Of course, the network didn't talk about Asian Americans, probably thinking there weren't enough APA Nielsen families to bring in the big advertising bucks. Or maybe it remembered the *All-American Girl* fiasco. So ABC stuck to what it knows. The report, "America in Black and White," came complete with its own manufactured facts—I mean, poll. Here's the lead: "Americans—black and white alike—overwhelmingly agree that racism is a national problem."

Wow. Racism is a national problem! Stop the presses! It would be news if everyone thought we were a "colorblind" society.

But notice the inherent racism in the very first words of the lead, "Americans—black and white alike." Asians aren't American? Do we count at all? Nope. They didn't ask.

And whom do we root for? Blacks? Whites?

The closest we came to inclusion in the report was with the question, "Do you think blacks and other minorities are discriminated against in hiring or not?"

More whites said yes than you would have thought: 49 percent. Seventy-seven percent of blacks said yes. Five years ago, 86 percent of blacks said yes. A reduction, perhaps.

The follow-up question was, "Do you think blacks and other minorities should receive preference in hiring to make up for past inequalities, or not?"

The majority of whites (80 percent) and, for the first time in five years, the majority of blacks (56 percent) said no.

The answers can be explained in at least a couple of ways: the emergence of more successful blacks or the self-help attitudes of Farrakhan. Is that progress?

Imagine what ABC could have found if it had expanded its scope beyond black and white. Consider that in big cities like Los Angeles, Southeast Asians have replaced blacks as the preferred victims of discrimination. Over 40 percent live in poverty. Nearly 80 percent are dependent on welfare. By seeing only in black and white, ABC missed a bigger story as well as a chance to educate people on another misunderstood group—Asian Pacific Americans. We don't fit in a black-and-white model.

The American race situation is a lot more complicated than that. Old-style thinking is black and white. It won't help you in the diversity of 2000 and beyond. The world is colorized beyond even Ted Turner's wildest residual dreams.

The poll highlighted another point: blacks and whites, the main event in the race debate, are really quite ignorant of one another. Well, here's a news flash for both groups: If they don't learn about Asians (or Latinos for that matter) any time soon, the race situation in the U.S. is going to get a whole a lot worse.

And that's a big reason why Asian Pacific American Heritage Month has to be a bigger deal that it is. It's for us and them.

May 24, 1996

Have Another Holiday
What we have to celebrate on MLK Day

Martin Luther King Jr. Day has come and gone, and I'm sure there are more than a few Asians in America who are still wondering why they didn't get their mail on Monday.

Where did all those mail guys and gals go? Was MLK a postal worker who got everyone the day off? (Actually most people didn't get the day off, including me. That's because, to paraphrase Dr. King, "I may have a dream. But I definitely have a deadline.")

It's funny how for this fairly new holiday, it's already

become one of those days—like Veterans Day or Presidents Day—when the banks are closed, the parking laws don't apply, and the buses are late. But on purpose. Yet, many of us don't really know or appreciate exactly why. Not really.

It's an attitude that is all too prevalent among Asians. Holiday? What holiday? It's a black holiday, right?

Wrong.

Considering how most in the Asian community are recent immigrants, with an institutional memory that may go back to, say, Reagan, it's not uncommon to find people totally clueless when it comes to Martin Luther King Jr. or his achievements. After all, most of us come from societies where the color of people's skin is all the same. Asian immigrants really don't know how to fully appreciate Dr. King. In our home countries, there's no black and there's no white. Dr. King has no context. Did he march for us?

It's not even really a matter of knowing about Dr. King, or not. Children of Asian immigrants certainly get a rudimentary sampling of information about King in school. They know Dr. King as one of the few black people mentioned outside the Civil War in the curriculum who did not play sports. Even a citizenship class will flash a picture of King as a black hero, exposing adults to at least an icon of the man. But do the newcomers understand Dr. King's struggle and do they link that with the difficulties they have with their own lives as non-whites in America?

I doubt it.

When an Asian gets a job in an all-white institution, or is taken seriously by a bureaucrat, or not spit on or called "gook" by a bigot walking down the street, they rarely pay homage to Dr. King for helping move society toward greater recognition and inclusion of all people of color.

More than likely, the attitude is "What did Dr. King ever do for me?"

I was willing to accept this as symptomatic of newcomers to America; a part of their gradual Americanization. Maybe one day they'll see the link to Dr. King, perhaps on the day they encounter their first personal instance of discrimination. But to my surprise, this "Dr. King Who?" phenomenon isn't just limited to immigrants.

A recent poll taken in the San Francisco Bay Area seems to corroborate that notion. Residents were asked about their perceptions of the race problem. Was it a big problem? Apparently not. Only 13 percent of Asians said it was, compared to 29 percent of blacks, 30 percent of Latinos, and 18 percent of whites. At 35 percent, Asians were the largest group to describe race as a "small problem" or "no problem at all."

Is it any surprise that, to Asians, Dr. King might as well be some optometrist at the mall?

Recently, I found myself talking to a young Asian American. A smart, well-educated, American twenty-something. Sure, she knew about Dr. King. But as for what he meant in her life, Dr. King definitely was old news. Older than disco. He was history.

And the holiday? Just another day. No big deal. It's like Earth Day. Remember that novelty? To her, Dr. King was all in the past. Equal opportunity? She took that for granted. "I've got that," she said.

And what about affirmative action? She didn't need it. She knew her abilities. She knew she could compete, and get things on her own. "I'm not hung up about all those things," she told me. "Not like you folks from the '60s."

Oh yeah, when Dr. King had his big dream, I was

eight. And I knew it was important. Dr. King wasn't Filipino, but he was talking for us. It was this "folks from the '60s" thing that got to me more than anything else she said. The young lady had effectively put me in an old people's home, as if to remember Dr. King was passé. It made me wonder, if Dr. King were alive today, and the young lady was right about race, maybe he would have declared the defeat of racism and moved on to a new fight—ageism. After all, he'd be 69. Would "I have a dream?" be turned into "I need a nap?"

Still, the young woman's chilly response exposes a gap that exists not just between immigrant and native-born, but the gap that exists generationally between those who appreciate Dr. King's importance and those who don't; those who care even more 35 years after the "I Have A Dream" speech, and those who couldn't care less. Are we indeed in a new time in which Dr. King has become irrelevant?

I'd hate to think so. But it does seem that there is a tendency to turn Dr. King's day into modern nostalgia; Dr. King as a warm fuzzy memory instead of a vibrant reminder of the challenges still ahead. If his era has indeed come and gone, why does it feel to this observer that all people of color are still going uphill?

That's why it's important for Asian Americans to understand exactly what Dr. King means to us. Our community, more than 60 percent immigrant, is involved in a new struggle for power and acceptance. But our new fight is an old one, a newer version of battles waged in the '60s. When we forget that, we lose the moral and ethical base that gives power to all our hopes and dreams. We're out there by and for ourselves. That's not a winning strategy for the next millennium. It's certainly not in the spirit of Dr. King.

January 22, 1998

An Easter Vigil

Where Catholicism does and doesn't work

At some point this week, the media will treat us to an image from the Philippines. It will be a picture of a Filipino man carrying a cross on his way to be "crucified." It's about as close as you can get to a literal rendering of crucifixion while still maintaining the right to call it "symbolism." There might even be more than one person lined up, burdened with the heavy lumber and garbed for passion, right down to the crown of thorns. It's not some weird faddish thing. It's just another Holy Week activity in the wonderful world of Christianity.

To all those who seek crucifixion this year, let me just say, I admire your forthrightness a lot more than I admire those kooks who used to dress up to see the *Rocky Horror Picture Show.*

I'm not one of the zealots. Yet. But just this year, I've come to terms with my religious side. It's that part of me that's less amok, more contemplative. It's the side of me that recognizes the Big Picture and wants to ally my soul with something eternal.

So this year, I started going back to church.

"Church?" Yep. I started polishing my Sunday Shoes again.

Saying you go to "Church" is practically anathema to one who makes a living going amok. "Church" is for the quiet, submissive followers. It's not about the individual, the visionary, or the original thinker. It's about compromise, catechism, and rote thought. It's a place where an Asian can find a good bowl of dogma. Isn't it?

Not necessarily.

Certainly it's about God and prayer and spirituality; and do those subjects really have a place in the normal discourse of free men and women?

Well, they should. But more often than not, they don't. I know. I ignored these issues for a long time. I am what they call a "lapsed" Catholic. But I've discovered that nothing ever expires in the Catholic Church. You may let go, but they never do. My upbringing was both secular and religious. I was a public school kid who went to catechism and served as an altar boy. As many young people do, I began to question my upbringing while in college. Why was I baptized? Why wasn't I given a choice? I was just a baby, so the idea of "original sin" must have been a conspiracy, one that got me in the fold before I could digest solid foods.

Then there was the roots thing. As an Asian American, shouldn't I have "talent on loan from Buddha?" Shouldn't I have an Asian sense of my spirituality? As a descendant of immigrants from the Philippines, weren't my ties closer to the indigenous people, the so-called "pagans" and their natural gods? Or were the Muslims my natural spiritual allies?

Studying the history made me wonder whether honoring Catholicism was not antithetical to the truth of my heritage. Was I honoring the imperialistic Spaniards and their lackey missionaries who gave my family a new last name and new cultural baggage?

The roots issue made me wonder. But so did the sex issue. With any religion, there is always the sex issue. It didn't help that I was well into my "Gee, aren't Jewish women attractive" phase. And then the "Gee, aren't all the women in this diverse world attractive" phase. By then, I was totally turned off to both the New Testament and the Old Testament. I had my own testament going.

So what happened? I went to hell and back? No. It just seemed like that. The years went by. I left bachelorhood. I got married. I had kids. And except for a general preference for "good" versus "evil," I had no apparent spiritual beliefs.

Then one day, while on the road, I was looking for reading material in my hotel room. I picked up one of those ubiquitous things called the Gideon Bible. The Gideons were started by a group of traveling business-men who gathered while on the road to read the Bible. Now there are Bibles in hotel drawers worldwide.

When I picked up the book, I remember saying to myself, "It's just literature." That's the comforting cop-out. That means you're still in the realm of the sane and rational secular world. That's the realm of reason, not of faith. Heaven? What's that? We're in a world where two plus two equals four.

But as I read on, I realized I wasn't reading John Grisham, or Tom Clancy, though the Bible is actually quite racy and violent in parts. I'm sure Biblical scholars even have a complete body count, or at the very least know the number of references to the term "fornication."

As for me, I was astonished at how many of the passages I read resonated with some of my core beliefs. I could see the habit of my second grade nun, Sister Mary Bernadette. You see, the memory never completely fades. It's Catholicism's spiritual life-support machine. They won't let you turn it off. And now reading all the stories from the loaves and fishes to Lazarus rising from the dead, I too was coming back into consciousness.

Soon after that I went to my first confession in many, many years. We'll save that for another column. For now, let's just say that my penance did not exceed 50,000 "Our Fathers," and 50,000 "Hail Marys." Part of my penance was setting a good example for my kids. So of course, they were all recently baptized.

And on Sundays, we do "Church." In fact, we do every-thing short of crucifixion. I've discovered that

"Organized Religion" is not "Organized Crime." The Pope may be hard to take at times, but I still have a long way to go before reaching full "heretic" status.

I still question many things about the Church and God. Church I have come to see as more than a building. It's a community. And as for God, well, I don't involve myself in proving God exists. That's a fool's quest. I can't prove it. But that doesn't mean he doesn't exist. Frankly, I pity the either/or types who are as rigid in their belief in rational knowledge as the most seething religious zealot. The late Carl Sagan, the scientist and author, comes to mind.

In a recent issue of *Newsweek*, Sagan's wife, Ann Druyan, says at the time of his death there was no deathbed conversion. "No appeals to God, no hope for an afterlife."

Druyan said Sagan never wanted to believe. "He wanted to know."

Many like Sagan hold true to one world or the other. But I don't believe in such mutual exclusivity. I believe because I want to know. There must be a point where the secular and the religious meet.

Of course, as a person of color, I have other issues as well. And I have not fully settled the conflict between what missionaries did and my indigenous "Filipino-ness." Of course, I can blame man for that one. But accepting Catholicism as part of the evolution of the Philippines also kept me from praying to the Comet Hale-Bopp and the lunar eclipse.

The other issue is my amok state, the constant battle I feel people of color have with a society that too often chooses to ignore them. But I've figured out how spirituality and my amokness go hand in hand. Since many of the things discussed in this column are based on a moral sense of right and wrong, there's no contradiction.

Spirituality only provides a more reliable compass to the amok. It only fuels the rampage.

March 28, 1997

Happy Kwanzamok!

A modest proposal for a holiday of our own

The other night I wore a Santa hat. A Filipino Santa? Not since Marcos, some would say.

Granted, the red went well with my black hair, but there is still no more ridiculous sight than an Asian American wearing a Santa hat. It is incongruous, like saying, "Boy, look at that skinny elephant!" It just doesn't make sense. Not even as a fashion statement.

Though the original St. Nicholas was born 1,500 years ago in Turkey and can thus claim some Asian heritage, the popular image of Santa Claus works against us. This common Santa "look" was actually derived in America from Clement Moore's *A Visit from St. Nicholas*, which begins with the line, "'Twas the night before Christmas...."

As a poem, it was a tremendous device because despite specific language, there was no literal rendering. It was all in the mind. This was before television, before the Olson twins, before Warner Oland as Charlie Chan. People were allowed to have their own idea of Santa. Perfect for the diverse America of the early 19th century.

But leave it to the existing media to spoil it all. Thomas Nast, the American illustrator whose famous cartoons pilloried Boss Tweed and Robber Barons, took the poem and created a drawing for Harpers Weekly in the 1860s. The rest, as they say, is history. Santa became fixed in people's minds as a total "look." Fat white man. Beard as white as snow. Rosy Cheeks. Cherry Nose. Reindeer fetish.

He's not us. Too much hair. Too much red. Talk about cultural imperialism.

Santa is an American creation, and it's fueled the holiday commercialism ever since. People are browbeaten into excessive gift buying, egged on by His Fatness. For example, take that odious practice of "stocking stuffers." I frankly like to give small, meaningful gifts. Instead, those of us who prefer small presents are made to feel like puny cheapskates in this "bigger is better" world. What do you mean, "Thanks for the 'stocking stuffer'?" That's your gift, buddy. And you know where you can stuff it.

We need an antidote to all this. We need to create a skinny man with no beard who will knock some sense into us. And I am that man.

We need to create our own Asian American holiday. And I have just the right model. Kwanzaa.

"Kwanzaa?" you ask? "Is that Japanese—like Gyoza? Or is that African American? And if so, what will the neighbors say?"

The neighbors will thank you for bringing some sanity to the holidays.

Kwanzaa was created by Dr. Maulana Karenga, chair of the Black Studies Department at Cal State Long Beach in 1966. Based on African harvest celebrations, it spans the seven days between Christmas and New Year's Day.

The word Kwanzaa means "first fruits" in Swahili. The weeklong celebration revolves around Nguzo Saba, or seven principles. They are Umoja, or unity; Kujichagulia, or self-determination; Ujima, or collective work and responsibility; Ujamaa, or cooperative economics; Nia, or purpose; Kuumba, or creativity; and Imani, or faith.

But never mind the Swahili. These are values that are important in any culture. Even Asian American culture.

Take the principle of unity, for example. Filipinos are

the largest Asian American group in California. Yet, ask any Filipino which term they identify with and few will say Asian American. While Asian American Heritage Month in May has helped to foster some identity in America, it sometimes comes off as a big carnival showcase for hula dancers and dragon heads. The spiritual element of Heritage Month is empty. Kwanzamok to the rescue.

Kwanza-what? In the spirit of pirated icons, celebrations, and cultural cross-fertilization, the time has come to celebrate our own brand of holiday—KwanzAA (the AA could stand for Asian American). Or in honor of me, its creator, call it Kwanzamok!

In fact, all seven principles of KwanzAA provide Asian Americans with worthwhile starting points for annual reflection. This is the time we assess what we've done, and what's left to be done.

Self-determination is related to our political involvement. Have we participated fully in our society as a whole? What have we done to let our voices be heard?

Collective work or responsibility is connected to our sense of community involvement and assisting other Asian Americans. Have we done what we can to help others?

A corollary to this is cooperative economics. What can we do to invest in each other to create businesses and jobs that help our immediate community and the community at large?

Purpose is about identifying common values for all Asian Americans. Why must we create an Asian American identity? Why must we work together politically and economically?

Creativity is about our hulas and dragon dances. Why do we dance, speak, and act as we do?

Faith concerns our respect and tolerance for all of our

212

spiritual beliefs. Some kneel. Some sit in lotus positions. Some take their orders from a man called Moon. Some prefer cash.

And let's not forget the rituals that mark all great holidays. Since Kwanzaa celebrates a harvest, Kwanzamok can be a harvest of ideas and feelings of the past year, hopes and desires for the new year. Each night, a scented candle is lit for each principal, and small token gifts are given to children. A book. Or, if you must, any small toy not made by exploited child or prison labor in Asia.

Kwanzamok will span essentially the same time as Kwanzaa, the period between Dec. 26 and Jan. 1, a time usually considered a void after Christmas. But while Kwanzaa is seven days, Kwanzamok will be eight days (eight being a lucky number for Asians).

On the sixth day, Dec. 31, we'll celebrate and light firecrackers as others will that night. This will be our amok night, when we let it out.

On the seventh day, Jan. 1, we'll avoid football and reconsider our hangovers.

And finally on the eighth day, Jan. 2, we'll have our symbolic feast. This is based on the food that all Asian American culture share in common, whether they call it lumpia, or imperial roll, or egg roll, or whatever. Each day we'll gather an ingredient for our lumpia—the wrapper, cabbage, carrot, tofu, parsley, etc. We'll roll it all up and share our lumpia with everyone we see, passing them out like cigars.

It ain't politically correct. It's my own version of the great Kwanzaa, Filipino-style—Kwanzamok. Now take that Santa hat off.

December 20, 1996

213

14

Our Race Future

No Gingrich in the Politics of Inclusion

I'm in shock. This is better than impeachment. Newt's been neutered. I shed no tears.

Four years ago, he nearly wrecked my life.

In '94, I was "Gingriched."

I had been a talk host at San Francisco's KSFO radio, newly purchased by ABC. Young hosts like me were given orders to help make the station the new, hip, "youthful" talk power in the Bay Area.

It didn't happen. We were given all of 17 weeks.

I had left opportunities in Washington, D.C., moved my family from east to west, only to run into what should have been a fairly routine situation — mid-term election politics.

But it wasn't routine. It was the most polarizing of campaigns. Cheered on by angry rhetoric, Republicans took over with landslide victories. Democrats lost seats in the House and Senate. Chairmanships were handed over to the GOP. Statewide, Prop. 187, the proposal to strip social services from illegal immigrants, was all the rage. White rage, to be precise.

Within a month of the election, KSFO fired us all.

"You're too liberal," they said, "and we're going conservative."

The bosses were interpreting a short-term political trend as a "commercial" trend. Nice guys were out. An "in your face," outrageous incivility was "in." The "never before spoken," the "best left unsaid," was now blurted out with regularity.

It seemed bound to happen. Rush Limbaugh had already made the tack popular. The '94 election only sealed it for management. Soon, stations throughout the country began cloning "Rush" with their own local versions of vitriolic, edgy, ultra-conservatives. The political trend became a radio format. It was called "conservative, hot talk." Others called it by a more truthful moniker: "hate radio." It was talk radio's new meal ticket. Meanwhile, moderate to liberal talk hosts like myself were treated like illegal immigrants.

But, as they say, how times have changed.

Four years later, the radio station that fired me may not be smart enough to hire me back, let alone admit that so-called "hate radio" has peaked.

But it better realize that the "hate politics" that inspired their hot talk is dead.

The '98 midterms prove it's time to shred that "Contract with America." America wants a new deal.

Certainly, politicians who don't see the trend will no longer be politicians. And the trend is right under their noses. All they have to do is follow the demographics.

California is currently 51% white. In the next few years, the tremendous growth will occur among Latinos and Asians. Blacks will be steady at 9% of the population. But all together throughout the state, minorities will be the majority in 20 years, even sooner in larger cities. By 2050, it will be the state of the nation.

The smart ones are picking up on the trend now. How

216

does a politician build a 20 percentage point win like Gray Davis?

Move to the center and don't demonize ethnic communities. Lead with grace and compassion. Put away the flamethrower.

In '94, led by Gingrich, the GOP went to the extremes. Look at the backlash this mid-term. According to the Field Institute's exit polls, Latinos went for Davis over Lungren, 75-20 percent. Blacks were for Davis by 83-11 percent. Asians were for Davis by 66-32 percent.

Moving to the center certainly worked for Sen. Boxer. Trailing challenger Matt Fong just weeks ago, Boxer pulled off a stunning double-digit winning margin. The tide turned when news reports revealed a Fong donation to an extreme, right-wing, anti-gay organization. It was so right wing, it made ultra-liberal Boxer look like a centrist!

It was feared that the angry white male vote that catapulted Gingrich would hurt Boxer. But this time around it was neutralized by the "Angry Ethnic Voter." The Field Institute's numbers had Latinos for Boxer over Fong by 71-23 percent. Blacks were 85-13 percent. Boxer even won Asians 51 percent-46 percent.

Fong may have banked on winning blind support from Asian voters. Some did choose to vote color over substance. In San Francisco, the Chinese Voter Education Committee's exit polling shows 66 percent of Chinese voters went for Fong. Then they switched by a 3-1 margin to vote for Gray Davis.

But that crossover wasn't enough to catapult Fong. Fong didn't need just ideological crossover. He needed ethnic crossover, especially Latino. He should have been going to more barrio lunches and selling his family values in Spanish. The "mama's boy" trick may have worked in the Latino community.

Such are the miscalculations by those unwilling to embrace the politics of a multi-cultural America.

Back to Gingrich. On a national level, it was becoming too obvious that he was just the wrong man, and the wrong style for our new time. How long do you think white rage will play to an electorate that's turning browner and yellower every day? Voters are more ethnic than ever, and they're just beginning to recognize their collective power.

Republicans realize that their abandoned "Big Tent" notions of the GOP are better than pitching a lean-to on the White House lawn. The Bushes know it. They were big winners in Texas and Florida.

"This is a victory of inclusion," said Jeb Bush, at his Florida victory speech, standing in front of a podium of Blacks, whites, and Latinos.

It's the second coming of his dad's "Kinder Gentler" Republicanism. George Bush's sons certainly seem intent on not committing Republican sins of the recent past. After years of being Limbaughed and Gingriched, voters like a more moderate style.

Now the fight is for a center big enough to hold us all.

So forget the wedges and the hate rhetoric. Turn off the hate talk on the radio. The trend is toward inclusion. The real revolution in American politics wasn't Gingrich's short-term white rage of '94. It's the emergence of a multicultural political awareness. It's more than the politics of a New California. It's the politics of a New America.

November 9, 1998

218

The Death of Asian America?

1 998 ends with one bomb blast after another. It's eye
rolling time in America: Impeachment. Infidelity.
Iraq — I.I.I.

In "panic-speak" that's pronounced, *"Ai-yai-yai!"*

On the eve of the sex-lies impeachment debate,
Clinton wags the House, choosing to bomb Iraq based on
a UN inspector's report. It delays the debate just one
day. Then, in another surprise, House-speaker elect Bob
Livingston (R-Louisiana) does a pre-emptive strike on
the media by announcing he's strayed from his own marriage on several occasions. But, as he points out, at least
he wasn't having sex with staffers on his payroll. How
comforting.

What else could House Republicans do? Why, give the
man a standing ovation! What an honorable, unimpeach-
able guy! (The fourth GOP sex infidel in recent memory).
What hypocrisy! (He'll make a great Congressional
leader). Now let's defile the constitution, go against the
popular majority, and get rid of the real sex liar!

Yes, this country is in deeper trouble than we all
think. So let me drop another bomb on you.

If you honestly don't care about any of the first part of
this particularly amok column, then 1999 may spell the
beginning of the end for Asian America.

Hyperbole? It's hard to overreact when the U.S. House
votes to impeach a President.

The middle, where most Asian Americans find a comfortable balance, appears more volatile than ever.
While I feel race is more important than ever, as evi-
denced by demographics, we must gradually acknowledge our role in non-ethnic terms. We're here. We're
Americans. If we can't get upset over an impeachment

process dictacted by the vengeance of the extreme right, then maybe the change in American politics will take place without us. Ignore it and be ignored.

The issue came up as a colleague asked me about Jay Kim, the disgraced Korean American voted out of Congress in November.

In an unintentional way of self-marginalization, some see his final vote in the impeachment debate as our only "Asian American angle."

Yet, focusing on Jay Kim is like concentrating on the fly rather than the horse poop.

Let's not totally dismiss the importance of the Kim story. He may be a fly in the impeachment story, but in his own drama, Kim is his own pile of poop.

Like it or not, Jay Kim is more representative of the emerging Asian American community than anyone cares to acknowledge. He represents the growing split between the Asian immigrant and the native-born Asian American. He represents the best and worst of us.

On the surface how can you not like Kim. He was the Horatio Alger immigrant who comes to America. Like many newcomers, he's aggressive and savvy, adept in business and high tech to gain respectability. He runs for Mayor and finds natural allies in the white conservative camp. For Kim, it was no less than the conservative stronghold in Southern California — Orange County. He runs for Congress and wins. He's the Korean Jimmy Stewart — Mr. Smith. But then his short term knowledge of America leaves him in the dark. Asian Americans? What's that? Civil Rights history? He became the immigrant who couldn't figure out which was the adjective, which was the noun in the phrase "Asian American." He thought he was a self-made American of his own design who could play both sides of the ocean. When the going got tough, he got nostalgic.

He sought campaign funds from South Korea — over $250,000 in illegal foreign and corporate donations.

Stupid? Arrogant? Criminal? All three? When Kim needed support, Asian Americans didn't know him. And the white right wing? They let him choke on his kimchee.

It's what happens when you think you're self-made in America--the invincible immigrant. Something always comes along to un-make you.

Had he not reacted to a natural alliance for his home-land, Kim could have still been in office today. Instead, he's working part-time for Webster's Dictionary — as an illustration for the word "pariah."

And is there any denying his downfall was his Asian-ness, his overweening reliance on "ethnicity"?

Now how is all this tied up with impeachment and the end of Asian America?

Just as Jay Kim relied on his ethnicity too much, maybe Asian Americans have too.

It was never genuine to begin with. Where is "Asian America," anyway? It's merely a political construct. Politicos created the term to give the mainstream a han-dle on us. Defined by ethnicity, the numbers start to add up: Filipino, Chinese, Japanese, Korean, Viet Namese, Indian, et al. We gain visibility. Maybe even power.

But what do we do on issues where our ethnicity is not the central factor, such as in impeachment? If there's no pigment on the issue, do we just shut up? Do we really need an "Asian American impeachment angle" to discuss the constitutional direction of OUR country? We are, after all, talking about us.

To declare it our business seems to break away from what has become a comfortable definition of "Asian America." It's a definition that only gives us relevance and standing on issues of race and ethnicity alone.

Go ahead, comment on immigration, hate crimes,

affirmative action — issues where race is everything. But when it comes to the tough question of the day — impeachment — it seems easier to duck and cover and save what little power we have for another day. If there is another day.

As I said ealier, politics is changing. Whenever we can talk of Iraq, impeachment and infidelity in the same essay, you know American politics is moving in a whole new direction. Even our pet issues are changing based on definitions from the far right. Matters of race and civil rights are falling to more homogenized notions of fairness and equality. Class factors are being added to race factors. If we merely define ourselves by race, then we're endangered of defining ourselves out of the political conversation.

If the new millenium is to start off any better than the old, when we smarted from the residual impacts of exclusion laws and old racist notions — then nothing short of total involvement in the national debate will do.

Why "ghettoize" our voice? If the term "Asian America" limits our issues, then the term is inadequate. What's more, any progress we've made will fade due to our self-limitations. To prevent that we must embrace the idea of a "New Asian America" — an Asian American perspective that goes beyond race and ethnicity, that lets the mainstream know we are more than a special interest. We have American interests.

The politics of our day demand that we change. But a change requires the guts and imagination to know a real Asian American issue when we see one.

December 18, 1998

Unbecoming in the Senate

Thank goodness for Hawaii! Because of its stalwart duo of veterans in the Senate — senators Dan Akaka and Dan Inouye — Asian Americans will have a role in the impeachment trial, even if it only means being in the room.

That's still better than all other minority communities combined, many of which boast wide popular support for Clinton. They don't get any real representation at all. Akaka and Inouye are essentially carrying the load for people of color all over ethnic America.

It wouldn't be that way, if the Senate were as they say, a little more "diverse."

Go ahead, take a good look at the U.S. Senate. Ask yourself if it looks anything like the America of the new millennium.

The body that will decide on the removal of William Jefferson Clinton from America's highest office actually resembles the board rooms of the most elite Fortune 500 companies.

With some exceptions — even a handful of Fortune 500 companies have some African Americans on them.

The Senate is different. It's the boardroom of the United States. And just look at the makeup of its "brilliant mosaic":

The Senate has no African Americans.

The Senate has no Latinos.

As they say, zero, zip, nada, wala, bupkis. In any language, it's a bust.

Oh, let's not forget, there is one American Indian — Ben Nighthorse Campbell, the Democrat turned Republican from Colorado.

But aside from the turncoat Democrat, there are the

two Asian Pacific Americans Akaka and Inouye, and that's it for people of color.

Three out of 100. Not bad, if only the country were 97 percent white. We wouldn't allow any other public institution to be so lopsided.

Just to make yourself feel better, go ahead and count up the 9 women who are senators, all of them white. They count as "minorities" in a pinch. But can you really feel all that good with women holding just nine percent of the 100 seats in the Senate? Lack of pigmentation is one thing, but these mind-numbing Senate testosterone levels should give everyone chills.

Now contrast the parallel world of the white proxies in the Senate to my home state, California.

In the Golden State, updated figures show that the so-called minority populations will be the majority even earlier than first reported. Not in 2025, as is expected nationwide. And not in 2006. How does the year 2001 grab you?

People are beginning to see diversity in all its glory from the delivery room to the State House. On the week Cruz Bustamente was sworn in as the state's Lieutenant Governor, "Jose" was reported as the most popular boy's name in California, topping the traditional Robert, James, Michael, David, and John.

The signs are all there. And of course, this New California is really just the new America. It all makes one wonder just who exactly is being represented by the rich white boy's club called the Senate.

Notice the touch of class in the phrase "rich white boy's club." We already know how white and male it is, but let's not overlook "rich." Common Cause, the Washington-based lobbying group,puts the number of millionaires in the Senate at 40 percent. No doubt, one gets a tremendous advantage from being wealthy in the

Senate. For a six-year term, a Senator must raise around $5 million just to run a competitive campaign. That's a price tag that tends to limit participation.

But "rich white male" isn't nearly as offensive as when you add the descriptive term "old." That's where Asian Americans, particularly Filipino Americans, can bristle a bit. Add "old" to the mix and there's a certain paternal quality present that brings to mind the American colonial mentality that many Filipino immigrants still feel. Did we make a mistake in choosing Mr. Clinton? Don't you worry, little brown brothers, here are the old white Senators to come and make everything better.

This is where commentators and pundits get chills down their spines over the solemnity and majesty of government. People go backwards in time and put an overwhelming reliance on the "Founders," the ultimate white people.

But it's the only way to justify the exclusive club that will decide whether Bill Clinton shall continue as our President.

One cannot expect fairness in a process that pretends to be legal, but in fact is political. Comparing impeachment to anything remotely resembling the legal system will get you nowhere. It's not really a "trial." But it is. The senators aren't really "jurors." But they are. What does that leave us? Probably with something short of "justice."

In the meantime Republicans say they're just following the constitution, all the while doing everything they can to embarrass and weaken the president.

But even the Clinton bashers know they can only go so far. Without the votes to remove the president at this time, they can only get away with whacking Clinton publicly for 24 hours, according to the new rules. Knowing that ahead of time, the whole process takes the form of an elitist frat house hazing, only far more serious and sinister.

It seems like a waste, considering that the only winner who will emerge more than likely will be the first senator with the guts to call it quits as soon as possible. That's the person who will go down in history as the real hero in this mess.

If only the political class had the good sense to rely more directly on the people to decide Clinton's fate — instead of letting our white proxies have at it in the Senate. But that's just it. The people have decided on Bill Clinton already. Twice.

Now we get a different kind of choice. Which do you really prefer: The rabid, politically self-serving nature of the House's partisanship? Or the Senate's stuffy, elite, white paternalism? No wonder the politics of the day seem so unbecoming.

January 11, 1999

Chinese Whine

White males have finally met their match in the victimhood derby. They're nothing compared to the new best whiners—San Francisco's Chinese Americans.

Five years ago, Patrick Wong was a 15 year old denied admission to the city's prestigious all-academic Lowell High School. The stated reason: it was full — of Chinese.

Discrimination?

Well, no. Since 1983 San Francisco has been under a court decree. The NAACP had charged black students were getting a raw deal by the city. To remedy any imbalance, court ordered desegregation divided up the city's 60,000 students into nine racial categories and put limits on individual schools: No more than 45 percent of any one group at any given school, with representation from at least four ethnic groups. The consent decree also provided the district over $300 million to address academic performance for black and Latino children. It all had a ring of logic to it, even if it wasn't always convenient.

It wasn't for Patrick Wong's mother Charlene Wong Loen, who wanted her son to go to Lowell. Desegregation be damned. She joined others in a massive class action to challenge the order. As luck would have it, her timing was impeccable. Affirmative action is on the ropes. California's Prop. 209 figurehead Ward Connerly is taking his message across the nation. People are tired of the old methods in dealing with race, if they even care at all. The political will is blowing toward Connerly. The legal will nearly gone. Settlement, anyone?

Despite what the lawyers are saying, the settlement is not one that benefits every kid in the city. It's a stop-gap. A short term measure that puts off the real problem of addressing the seemingly unreachable goal of equal opportunity in public education.

The settlement prohibits San Francisco schools from assigning any student to "a particular school, class or program on the basis of race or ethnicity, except as related to the language needs of the student."

If racial balance is the goal, the job has just been made all that more difficult. Now not only do administrators have both hands tied behind their back, they're blindfolded to boot. S.F. Schools Superintendent Bill Rojas may as well be walking a plank.

The NAACP can go back to the courts if any one school's balance goes out of whack. But this stipulation alone makes the whole "colorblind" remedy suspicious. They'll be back in court before your take-out order is ready. With race thrown out as a consideration, it's just a matter of time before the Asian American population

227

at Lowell reaches 60-70-80 percent. In the past the U.S. as a society decried all-white institutions. Are all-Chinese public institutions really any better?

And it couldn't have been reached without the willingness and determination of the Chinese plaintiffs. They were the "best public victims," those high scoring "A" students who were denied admission to Lowell High. Better than any group of aggrieved white males.

The whole situation spawned a weird corollary to the "model minority" idea that's been used against Asian Americans. Call them the "Denied Chinese-Americans of Lowell (henceforth, DCALs)." They've been the model minority key talking point of affirmative action foes. Newt Gingrich used to bring them up publicly as the poor victims of social engineering.

DCALs shouldn't feel victorious, just used. The settlement doesn't install their dream of a meritocracy based on grades and test scores. Racial and ethnic diversity is still a goal. You just can't use race. And it doesn't necessarily admit any more DCALs.

In fact, the DCALs may have shot themselves in the book bag. The new "class-based" plan San Francisco Unified is exploring will likely benefit poor Asians, not the mostly middle-class DCALs.

That leaves DCALs out in the cold, just as before. Maybe, they should celebrate their "whiteness" instead of the settlement. They've taken themselves out of a "race/ethnicity" context, and placed themselves in a totally new one. In the past, this was called "assimilation." But they've done it in such a drastic way with their color-blind stand. Where are they in other matters of discrimination? Blind as well? Or only when it suits them?

This is what happens when a sense of balance between private desires and the public good is lost in the community. Equal opportunity? Just for me, thank you. The

DCALs wanted it all, and they didn't seem to care about anyone else. Their whining carried the day. And it gave the angry white male — the natural opponents to affirmative action — a new public face.

As the city fulfills the settlement terms, look for some fallout. Don't think black and Latino communities didn't notice.

Even more significant may be the fallout within the national Asian American community. It threatens to expose the existing holes in the artificial umbrella of a coalition we know as "Asian America." When the Chinese went rogue on the Lowell issue, it was no different than a Clarence Thomas speaking out against the black civil rights mainstream.

One wonders what could have happened if the DCALs weren't so easily used and manipulated. Wouldn't it have been better if Chinese Americans had just pressured San Francisco into providing more Lowell-type magnet schools? More Lowells for everyone, and not "just Lowell for me." Unfortunately, the DCALs unwisely chose self-interest. And in the long run, it may have ended up costing us all.

February 22, 1999

ABOUT THE AUTHOR

EMIL GUILLERMO IS AN INDEPENDENT JOURNALIST, commentator, and humorist. He has many years of experience as a radio and television news anchor, interviewer, and talk host. Currently, he is host and executive producer of NCM: New California Media, a syndicated program of news and analysis on public broadcasting stations in San Francisco and Los Angeles

Guillermo's weekly column in *AsianWeek* also appears regularly in the *Honolulu Star Bulletin*, the *New York Filipino Express*, and Seattle's *Filipino Herald*. He has also written for the *San Francisco Examiner*, the *San Francisco Chronicle*, the *Oakland Tribune*, the *Los Angeles Times*, the *Washington Post*, *USA TODAY*, the *San Diego Union-Tribune*, the *Seattle Post-Intelligencer*, and *A. Magazine*. Guillermo's satirical column on the ethnic experience, "Amok," is a monthly feature of *Filipinas* Magazine.

As a television reporter, Guillermo's work has been seen nationally on NBC-TV and CNN. In 1989, after seven years as a reporter at San Francisco's KRON-TV, Guillermo became the co-host/anchor of National Public Radio's All Things Considered.

In Washington, D.C., Guillermo also served as the Press Secretary and speechwriter to former Congressman Norman Mineta. He lectures frequently at colleges around the country.

Born and raised in San Francisco, Guillermo graduated from Lowell High School, then Harvard, where he was a Lampoon member and went amok while delivering the Ivy Oration as class humorist.